P9-DCL-813

RACING TO THE FINISH

RACING TO THE FINISH

MY STORY

DALE EARNHARDT JR.

WITH RYAN MCGEE

W PUBLISHING GROUP

AN IMPRINT OF THOMAS NELSON

© 2018 DEJ Management, LLC

All rights reserved. No portion of this book may be reproduced, stored in a retrieval system, or transmitted in any form or by any means—electronic, mechanical, photocopy, recording, scanning, or other—except for brief quotations in critical reviews or articles, without the prior written permission of the publisher.

Published in Nashville, Tennessee, by W Publishing, an imprint of Thomas Nelson.

Thomas Nelson titles may be purchased in bulk for educational, business, fund-raising, or sales promotional use. For information, please e-mail SpecialMarkets@ ThomasNelson.com.

Any Internet addresses, phone numbers, or company or product information printed in this book are offered as a resource and are not intended in any way to be or to imply an endorsement by Thomas Nelson, nor does Thomas Nelson vouch for the existence, content, or services of these sites, phone numbers, companies, or products beyond the life of this book.

ISBN 978-0-7852-2160-9 (HC)
ISBN 978-0-7852-2196-8 (eBook)
ISBN 978-0-7852-2669-7 (SE)

Library of Congress Cataloging-in-Publication Data

Library of Congress Control Number: 2018949131

Printed in the United States of America

18 19 20 21 22   LSC   10 9 8 7 6 5 4 3

*To my wife, Amy Earnhardt, who gave me
strength, support, and Isla Rose.*

CONTENTS

FOREWORD

I first met Dale Earnhardt Jr. in 2012 when he was worried and anxious to return to the racecar. When I saw him again in 2016, he was riddled with physical and emotional symptoms from his multiple concussions, petrified and desperate to simply return to life.

Recovering from his injuries took tremendous effort and commitment, all in the face of overwhelming pressure to return to his beloved sport. He is one of the hardest-working patients I have ever treated. He worked tirelessly on his rehabilitation. It quickly became obvious to me that we were not only treating Dale and his injury but also the incredible forces surrounding his desire to please his fans, his family, his owners, and his legacy.

Dale has a strong tendency to think of others before thinking of himself. The title of this book, *Racing to the Finish*, is an interesting choice, as the decision of whether to retire played a ubiquitous role in every aspect of his care and outcome. I recognized that very early with Dale, but as I told him so many times, my only priority was for him to feel normal again. The rest would take care of itself.

As a clinician in charge of his care, I never really worried about the return-to-racing issue; I was much more focused on his living his life without the burden of and hypervigilance about his debilitating symptoms. Fortunately, we were successful in that regard. Yes, Dale faced many challenging moments, but I was always extremely confident that our treatments would prove effective and that he would get to the finish line. The fact that Dale recovered and returned to racing before retiring "on his own terms" (what I told him so many times) makes me so proud. Even more important is that Dale walked down the aisle symptom-free and married Amy, the love of his life.

In typical Dale fashion, the primary reason he is bravely sharing his story is for others to receive help with their similar injuries. Concussions afflict millions of pediatric, adult, geriatric, and military patients. During a typical day at our clinic at the University of Pittsburgh Medical Center (UPMC), we will see dozens of children and adults who are suffering from chronic symptoms and dysfunction associated with concussion. The majority of these individuals have not received any targeted treatment for difficulties that directly affect physical, social, vocational, and psychological functioning, even though we now agree as a field that concussion is a *treatable* injury. You'll read in this book about our UPMC model that reveals six different clinical profiles, or types, of concussions. Each of them requires active and targeted treatments to improve outcomes. We have and will continue to publish research proving the efficacy of this model.

As you will see from Dale's treatment, the field of concussion has evolved dramatically over the past few decades. The days of dark rooms and complete rest following this injury are being replaced with active physical therapies and targeted treatments that allow recovery to fully occur. Unfortunately, the science and evidence-based information represent a collective whisper buried in the cacophony of sensationalized and overwhelming media attention that leads to misinformation and a misunderstanding of concussion. As our recently commissioned Harris Poll indicated, 25 percent of parents prevent their children from playing sports because of concerns of concussions; a large majority of US adults believe you can only lessen symptoms and that you never fully recover; and they are not comfortable that they would know the steps to manage and treat a concussion if they sustained one.[1]

Dale's story is a call for action and change. Progress is being made, and Dale is a living testament to that. He has shared his story to better educate those who have experienced this injury and to accurately share that effective treatments are available. Even prior to this book, his story was making a difference. Many patients have told me they sought treatment at our clinic after hearing about Dale's case and recovery.

I am grateful to our incredible team at UPMC, including our researchers, athletic trainers, physical therapists, and treating clinicians. I also want to thank Dr. Petty, who delivered exemplary care to Dale and referred him to our clinic. Dr. Petty and I spent many hours in person and on phone calls working together to get Dale back in his racecar and back to life. He is such a caring and incredibly talented clinician. I also want to thank Kelley, Dale's sister, for her support, as well as Rick Hendrick for providing the free rein to allow Dale to recover fully. Rick's sole motivation was to see Dale healthy and well, and I truly respected that. And finally, Amy was unwavering and tough, a formidable assistant when it came to Dale

---

1 University of Pittsburgh Medical Center, "How Knowledgeable Are Americans About Concussions? Assessing and Recalibrating the Public's Knowledge," September 2015, http://rethinkconcussions.upmc.com/wp-content/uploads/2015 /09/harris-poll-report.pdf.

completing his physical therapies. She provided constant love and support during his recovery. I can see how they are a perfect fit for each other. I will never forget the personal text I received from Dale following little Isla Rose's birth. He was so grateful and full of pride and joy. Dale's moving on with his life as a family member, husband, and father is what this was all about all along.

Congrats on your recovery, Dale, you earned it. It was an absolute privilege to work with you.

Dr. Michael "Micky" Collins
Director, UPMC Sports Medicine
Concussion Program
June 2018

A LIFT, A SECRET, AND A PROMISE

Sunday, May 4, 2014
Talladega Superspeedway

We were having a good day at Talladega, NASCAR's biggest, most intimidating racetrack. If you know anything about my NASCAR career, then you know that me and that place, we've always had a special relationship. I won there six times. My father won there ten times. The Earnhardts and Talladega, we've grown up together. There's a whole generation of fans down there who were raised to root for me, taught by the generation before them, who rooted for my dad.

So whatever I did when I raced at Talladega was always a really big deal, good or bad. If the grandstand felt like I was making a move to the front, they would lose their minds. Even with forty-plus cars out there roaring around, I could hear them cheering. If they felt like I had been done wrong, I could hear them booing too. I loved it.

On this day, I had them rocking a couple of times. We led a bunch of laps and spent nearly half the day running up inside the top ten. Now, late in the race, they were waiting on me to make my move. So was my team in the pits, especially my crew chief, Steve Letarte. Just a few months earlier we'd won the Daytona 500. But for whatever reason we had never won together at Talladega. Today we really believed we had a chance to fix that.

But now, late in the race, I was stalled. We made a pit stop for fuel and I got stuck in the pack. I was boxed into my position with nowhere to go. With eight laps to go, I was setting up for my move to the front, but a slower, underfunded car moved in front of me.

At Talladega, you have to have a dance partner to team up with, to split the air, slip through it, and move up through the pack. But this car in front of me now, this was a bad dance partner. There was no way I could push that car to the front. Heck, there was no way I could push any of these cars around me to the front. I was jammed up, running three-wide in basically a 200-mph parking lot with nowhere to go.

I started doing the math in my head. How many laps were left? What was my running position? How many cars did I need to slide by to get back into the lead? I added all of that up and realized that the best I was going to do was get up into the top fifteen. Maybe.

So . . . I lifted.

I did. I backed off and got out of there. I jumped on the radio and I told my team that I thought there was going to be a big crash and I was staying back so I could stay out of it and steer around it when it happened. At Talladega we call it the Big One, when a pack of cars, just like the one I was running in right now, all wreck at once. Cars start spinning and there's smoke everywhere and you have no idea where you are going, what you are going to hit, or what's going to hit you. Even when you do think you're about to steer clear of it all, a car—or a wall—can come out of nowhere.

I didn't want any part of that. Not today. So, yeah, I lifted my right foot out of the throttle and I let my Chevy ease back out of that pack. I watched them all move out ahead of me and then made sure to give them their distance, but not too far. I stayed close enough that I could still hang on to their draft, staying on the back edge of that aerodynamic bubble that would keep me close, but not too close. There were twenty-seven cars on the lead lap, and I settled into twenty-sixth. If they started wrecking, I would have enough room and time to get around that mess without getting hurt.

To be clear, this is a strategy that a lot of drivers have used over the years, but they always did that at the start of the race, not with a few laps to go like I was doing. They hung back waiting to make a dramatic late move. I wasn't going to make any moves. My only move was to stay safe.

That was my whole goal. Don't get hurt. Not again.

There's a famous NASCAR story about Bobby Isaac, the 1970 NASCAR Cup Series champion. A few years later, in the middle of a race at Talladega, Bobby came over the radio and told his team to get a relief driver ready because he was getting out of there. He pulled down pit road, climbed from his car, and walked straight to a pay phone and called his wife. Bobby told her that a voice had spoken to him, clear as a bell, and told him to get out of the car. Earlier in that same race, an old friend of his, Larry Smith, had gotten killed. Bobby was done. He didn't race again that season and only ran Talladega one more time. Looking back, that was really the day that his Hall of Fame career ended.

Riding out those final few laps that day at Talladega, there weren't any mysterious voices in my head. The only voice I heard was my own. I felt awful about what I was doing. It went against everything that being a racer is about. I knew I was going to have to answer questions about it, not just from my fans but from my team. But none of them knew what I had been going through that month. No one did. Not even my fiancée, Amy.

They did know what I had endured nearly two years earlier, on August 29, 2012. Everyone did. During a tire test at Kansas Speedway I hit the wall going 185 mph and suffered a concussion that eventually forced me to get out of the car for two races later that season.

After I returned, everything went pretty much back to normal until one month before this Talladega race. On Monday, April 7, 2014, at the high-speed Texas Motor Speedway, I finished dead last after wrecking on lap 12. It was a bizarre situation. I was running down the frontstretch, blinded a little by the car in front of me, and my left front tire ran off the asphalt and into the infield grass. It was a mistake on my part, but it wasn't all that unusual. What was unusual was that it had rained all weekend and that patch of grass was like a mud bog. The way we were building our racecars, they rode super low to the ground. So, when I hit that soaked turf with a nearly two-ton machine at 200 mph, the grass grabbed that corner of my car and instantly folded it in. It bent that sheet metal and steel like it was nothing, like it was a cardboard box. It grabbed so hard my car actually went up in the air for a split second before slamming back down onto the blacktop. Now riding on only three tires, my car veered right and smacked the outside retaining wall, once . . . twice . . . three times . . . and then kind of dot-dot-dotted its way along the wall.

If you were watching that race on TV and saw my crash, you probably remember the fact that the car caught on fire. When I finally got the car stopped and climbed out over the hood, the whole rear end of my Chevy was up in flames. But you probably wouldn't have thought much of the size of all those impacts. If you're a race fan or a racecar driver, then you've seen or experienced hits just like that all the time.

For me, though, it was like an old wound had been opened. All of a sudden, my brain went back to showing symptoms I hadn't felt since 2012. They weren't as intense as what had forced me out of the car two years earlier; they were much subtler. But I knew something wasn't right. I knew it instantly.

I told no one. Amy knew I didn't feel well because she's the one who has to look after me every day, but I didn't share everything with her either. The only place where I exposed the true details of what I felt was in the notes app on my iPhone. The morning after the Texas crash, I opened that app and started regularly writing out the details of whenever I felt bad. I've been doing it ever since. A journal of symptoms.

At first, I don't think I even really understood why I started doing it. This sounds morbid, but when I look back now I realize that what I was doing was leaving a trail for others to discover in case something happened to me that kept me from being able to tell them myself.

I've never shared these notes with anyone until now. This is what I wrote in the days following that April 2014 Texas crash, just a few weeks before my decision to lift at Talladega. The notes start in the medical center at the racetrack, where every driver is required to visit following a crash, no matter how big or small, to be checked out by a doctor. From the track medical center it was home, then to a test session at Michigan Speedway, and then off to Darlington Raceway for the next event. These notes, the first I jotted down, are the vicious cycle I found myself living in after every hit on the racetrack:

Instantly in the infield care center I felt foggy. No pain or headache but felt a little foggy and quite a bit trapped.

Went home feeling a slight headache and visual issues like erratic eye movement. Not being able to focus on a single point or object. More than slight air-headedness or grogginess.

Spent night on couch with Amy. Got tired and went to bed. Felt trapped in my head some, but just slightly. Couldn't focus or remember simple things. Worried about my head all the time and couldn't plug into my surroundings.

Groggy head Tuesday AM, over 12 hrs after accident. Emotional frustrations then too.

Cleared up mostly by afternoon, 24 hrs after event. Felt almost 100% by dinner but was tired and ready for bed by 9.

Slept well and woke up feeling happy and solid. Hardly no worry about head. Plugged into all surroundings. Happy disposition. Wednesday by noon felt a-ok.

Wednesday noon, still some slight mental mistakes or slip-ups. Walked into a clear glass wall I thought was a door while focusing hard on racing mural, looking for my car in it. Could be a "throw it in the concussion bin" moment but I think it's still just a slight lack of mental sharpness that will be better by Friday.

Test session . . . both Tuesday and Wednesday, when I was in the car I felt sharper than when I wasn't. But when I drove on highway Tuesday with sunglasses I felt odd and not sharp. Removing sunglasses makes it much better.

5 pm Wednesday: test is done, felt solid in the car all day. Feel good now riding to airport. Have slight pressure pains in my head that last a second or two but really feel good and clear in my thoughts.

Thursday morning. Wake up at home with headache. Clear mind.

Had head pressure all day really.

Friday. First day 100% solid. By Saturday I have forgotten about any issues.

This all happened barely seven weeks after winning the Daytona 500. We'd started the season with three consecutive top-two finishes. The weekend before Texas I'd finished third at California Speedway. I was off to one of the best starts of my career, in my seventeenth full season in NASCAR's top division. We felt like we had a real shot at finally winning my elusive first season championship. There was no way I was going to let another concussion interrupt that.

Then, even after all of that trouble and worry at Talladega, I went to one of NASCAR's most challenging ovals, Darlington Raceway, and finished second. One week later I finished seventh at Richmond International Raceway.

It doesn't make much sense, right? My head is foggy for days and I'm walking into glass walls, but at the same time I'm testing at Michigan, one of our fastest racetracks, and running up front at Darlington at 170 mph? As I wrote in my notes, inside the racecar is where my brain and eyes actually felt the most normal. But when the symptoms started creeping back, so did those little pieces of worry. That little voice in the back of my still-healing brain, wondering if maybe I was one hit away from going right back to those dark days of 2012, the only time in my life when I was told I couldn't drive my racecar.

That's where my head was that day at Talladega. Yes, that racetrack was home to some of my greatest moments, but it was also home to most of the hardest hits of my career. In my mind, as I eased out of the throttle to lay back and ride out those final laps, that was me making a fair trade. I was bartering this race on this day so that I could run more races on other days. That's how I felt about it. Live to fight another day. Literally.

After the checkered flag I drove back into the garage. Just like after every race, my crew was waiting on me to help me out of the cockpit, chat about what happened, and then load up the truck to go home and get ready for the next race. Some of those guys on the No. 88 crew I had been with for years. They knew me. There was no faking it with us, so they knew what I had done. Steve Letarte did too. And I knew that they knew. I could barely look them in the eyes.

There's always a look of disappointment on everyone's faces when you have a bad finish, especially when you thought you had a real chance to win. But the looks on their faces were worse than just disappointment. They were mad, and they should have been. I couldn't take it. I just got out of there as fast as I could and headed home.

During that quick flight back to North Carolina I thought about those guys a lot. But mostly I thought about my fans, Junior Nation, and the constant desire to do right by them. I hear them all the time. "Go, Dale, go! Get up front! Stay up front! Go, go, go, man! Go as hard as you can all the time!" Which is great. It's what I'm there to do. But you know what? I can't do that if I'm hurt. I can't do that if I'm totally messed up because I tried to make something happen on a day when it wasn't really possible, trying to win a race that, honestly, I knew I wasn't going to win. Why would I try that at Talladega, the biggest, meanest racetrack, where it would be so easy for me to get hurt really bad?

NASCAR had a new championship format that, thanks to the fact that we'd already won a race, guaranteed us a spot in the post-season and a shot at the title in the fall. That meant that this race really didn't mean all that much. People had to know that, right? Did they not see me win the Daytona 500 just a couple of months earlier? There was no way they were really going to question my heart, right?

Wrong. They sure did. At least, that's what I've been told. That week I avoided social media, TV, and radio, anywhere I knew I might have to hear complaints about what I had done. As soon as I got home, I recorded an explanation for my *Dale Jr. Download* podcast, where I explained that I had made a mistake and I apologized for it. I said that I had tried to make an educated guess as to where and when the big crash would happen and I had misjudged it.

Some praised me for being so open and honest, for owning up to my mistake. Steve Letarte later said that he played that podcast for the crew, and when they heard me own up to it, they immediately stopped being angry with me. But the reality that I knew and that I had to live with was that I had only confessed to part of the truth. The whole story was in those notes, the ones I'd started taking just a few weeks earlier and would continue to write in secret for months and years to come.

Every single night that week after Talladega I lay wide awake in bed. I hated myself for what I had done, no matter what my reasons. That's not how you race. That's certainly not how an Earnhardt races. I made a promise to myself there in the middle of the night that I would never do that again. I decided that destiny, fate, God's plan—whatever you called it—it was going to happen to me the next day or the next race and, well, that's just what was going to happen to me. Period. There was nothing I could do about that, so there was no reason to keep worrying about it, certainly not to the point that I couldn't do my job. I let it go and it felt good. It was liberating, really.

I promised myself that I wouldn't lift my right foot again. I would race to win in every race I ran, just like I had always done before. I quietly made that promise to my team, my fans, my family, and to Amy as she slept right there beside me. I promised myself that I would never feel like this again. I was no longer going to be ashamed. I would be honest with my loved ones about how I felt. I would work to help others like me, silently suffering from head injuries, secretly keeping their own painful notes and living every day scared of what their futures might be.

I promised myself to keep the hammer down from that night forward, until whenever my driving career ended. I had no idea when that end was coming, but I knew, really for the first time, that it was coming sooner than later.

And I certainly had no idea how difficult the road to that finish line was going to be.

CHAPTER 1

HAMMERHEAD

I'm not going to tell my whole life story in this book. That's maybe for another day. But before we start down the road of how I got to the end of my racing career and how concussions played a role in reaching that end, I do think it's important that you get a little perspective. I want you to understand who I am, where I came from, and the world I grew up in. Once you know a little bit about that, then maybe the hows and whys of my reactions to my head injuries—and really everyone's reactions—might make a little more sense.

I love NASCAR racing. Always have, always will. And no matter how much I got beat up in a racecar, that was never going to change. Even if I had never been fortunate enough to become a racecar driver, I would've figured out some way to be around the garage. When I was a little boy, I played with Matchbox and Hot Wheels cars. Me and my buddies, we were always on a nonstop scavenger hunt. My dad would be out there racing and we would sneak around the garage all weekend collecting lug nuts, stickers, pieces of sheet metal ripped off of wrecked racecars, you name it.

Now, as an adult, I'm still playing with racing stuff. Let me put it this way: if you ever find yourself on eBay in the middle of the night thinking, *Man, who is this guy that keeps running up the prices on these old NASCAR programs and T-shirts and stuff? This dummy is paying way too much for this stuff!*—well, there's a really good chance that dummy is me. I'm the guy with a custom-built bar in his basement that's made from an old truck and wallpapered in classic racing stickers. Heck, man, I'm the guy who has a whole section of his property littered with wrecked machines that I've collected from friends to donate to the "Racecar Graveyard."

See? I love it. And I come by that honestly. My grandfather, Ralph Lee Earnhardt, was a NASCAR short-track legend. He was as old school as it gets. Like everyone else in Kannapolis, North Carolina, he started off working in the textile mill. Soon he took a second job working at a garage, and there he got a little taste of weekend short-track racing. He was hooked. So he quit his jobs and started spending all day and night working on his racecars in a little shop behind his house on Sedan Street. My Mammaw, Martha, still lives there.

Ralph chose to go racing for a living at a time when nobody did that. It worked out. He won hundreds of races, mostly on the short tracks of the Carolinas, and in 1956 he won a national championship in NASCAR's Sportsman Division, the beginning of what we now know as the NASCAR Xfinity Series.

My granddaddy was known for two things: his calm, levelheaded personality off the racetrack and his ability to kick your butt on the racetrack. He ran races nearly every night of the week, all while raising five kids, and did most of his racing close to home so he could take care of those kids. It seemed like nothing could slow him down. His motto, painted on some of his racecars, was

"Go or blow." His fellow racers gave him a nickname that kind of played off our last name, Earnhardt. They called him "Ironheart." Isn't that awesome?

Everything my grandfather did was watched like a hawk by his son, Ralph Dale Earnhardt. That's my dad. When Dad was a little boy, he would watch his dad work on those racecars behind the house. By the time he was ten years old, he was going to the track with my grandfather, where he and my great uncle would serve as the pit crew. Eventually, my uncles Randy and Danny joined them. The Earnhardts—all of them—were in the racing business, running sometimes four or five nights a week. Even Mammaw raced in the occasional "Powder Puff" races they held for the wives. One time she flipped Ralph's car onto its roof. Earnhardts are tough.

When my father was sixteen, he quit school. If you knew him, then you probably aren't surprised. School felt like it was in the way of what he really wanted to do, which was to go racing. Ralph, who hadn't finished school himself, was really disappointed. Dad always regretted that decision. They got on the outs with each other for a little while but eventually reconnected, and they did that through racing, Ralph helping Dale with advice.

They only actually raced together once. Dad loved to tell that story. Ralph was leading and Dad was running fourth, stuck behind a third-place car he couldn't pass. My grandfather came flying up there, and my dad thought his dad was just going to blow by and put him a lap down. Instead, Ralph Lee got up behind Ralph Dale and physically pushed him into third place. Dad said that third-place guy was so mad, complaining about "those Earnhardts."

That race they ran together was in 1972. My grandfather died of a heart attack in '73. He was only forty-five years old. Almost exactly one year later, Ralph Dale Earnhardt Junior was born. That's me.

Dad, like my granddad, was fully focused on racing. Sometimes maybe too focused. He was gone all the time, desperate to find race-cars to drive, and when he did find a ride he was desperate to make them do something big.

His reputation was way different from my grandfather's. Ralph was Mr. Even-Keeled. Dad was not. Not even close. He was cocky and stubborn and he didn't care one bit if you thought he was cocky and stubborn. So they gave him a nickname too.

"Ironheart" had been a compliment. What they started calling Dad was not, though it was still a play on words. They called him "Ironhead."

I don't care if it's your heart or your head or your entire body—if you were going to be a racecar driver when my grandfather and father came along, you had to be made out of iron. Racing seats were pretty much just regular old car seats. Seatbelts too. There were no head and neck restraints. The interiors of the cars were sparse and jagged. Helmets were tiny. Racetracks were lined with either bare concrete walls or metal guardrails just like you'd find on the local highway. They would run races, even on big speedways, when a car had ripped through the railing and sailed out of the racetrack into the parking lot, and what did they do? They just kept running. "Okay, guys, there's a big ol' hole in the fence up in Turn 2, and there's a bunch of metal sticking out all over the place up there. So . . . stay away from there. Cool? Cool."

Plenty of drivers were killed. Usually, that's how the racing world learned how to fix stuff. When NASCAR Hall of Famer Fireball Roberts died from severe burns suffered during a crash in the 1964 World 600 at Charlotte Motor Speedway, NASCAR mandated the use of rubber, puncture-resistant fuel cells. In the 1970 Rebel 400 at Darlington Raceway, Richard Petty barrel-rolled his car down the frontstretch, flinging the whole upper-half of his body in and out of the driver's side window on ABC's *Wide World of Sports*. I don't know how, but he was okay. Still, it spooked NASCAR enough to mandate the use of window nets to prevent that from happening again.

That's the world that my father and grandfather grew up in and raced in, and really, so did I. What doesn't kill you makes you stronger, right? Guys like Roberts and Petty and, yes, the Earnhardts—they all raced hurt, and they did it a lot. NASCAR's first champion, Red Byron, could barely use his right leg because of an injury suffered as a mechanic aboard a bomber during World War II. There was an explosion too close to the plane with the bomb bay doors still open, and it had filled Byron's leg full of shrapnel. So when he returned home after the war and wanted to resume his racing career, he bolted his leg brace to the clutch pedal. He's in the NASCAR Hall of Fame too. In 1984, Ricky Rudd, one of my father's longtime rivals, famously ran the Daytona 500 despite suffering big-time injuries at that same track just a few days before. His eyelids were completely swollen shut after violently rolling out of Turn 4. So what did he do for the big race? He got some duct tape and taped those swollen eyes open. The next weekend, wearing an army flak jacket to protect his cracked ribs, he won at Richmond.

In 1982, my father got into a wreck with Tim Richmond at Pocono Raceway, turned upside down, hit hard, and actually slid along the wall on his roof for what seemed like forever. He broke his leg, but he kept that to himself and never missed a race. Why? Because he remembered what happened in 1979, his rookie year in the Cup Series, when he wrecked at the same track and missed the next four races. The driver that subbed for him was NASCAR legend David Pearson, who won one of those four races. Dad was afraid he was going to lose the job he'd worked so hard to get. So, he made sure never to miss another race, even with that broken leg in '82.

In 1994 he broke a bone in his neck at Michigan, told no one, and went on to win his record-tying seventh championship. At Talladega in '96 he suffered a broken collarbone. The next week he had to get out of the car a handful of laps into the Brickyard 400 because the pain was just too bad. The man fans called "The Intimidator," a nickname he'd earned by being the toughest racer in the garage, nearly broke down crying on national TV when he saw his car drive off without him. The following weekend he refused to do that again, and he nearly won on the road course at Watkins Glen.

That was the mentality. You didn't get out of your racecar, no matter what. Broke a bone? Suck it up, man. Got your bell rung? Shake it off, take a headache powder, and get ready for the next race.

Racecar drivers are hardheaded. That's especially true when they are like me, the son and grandson of hardheaded racecar drivers! How hardheaded was I growing up? I was so hardheaded it inspired my father to give me a nickname that was the perfect sequel to what people had called him and his father before him.

He called me "Hammerhead," son of "Ironhead," grandson of "Ironheart."

When I started racing I earned that nickname pretty literally. People always ask me where I was when my father earned the greatest victory of his career, his slump-busting win in the 1998 Daytona 500. You know where I was? On the couch, at home in Mooresville, North Carolina, with a washcloth on my head. The day before I'd raced in the Daytona 300, the NASCAR Xfinity (then Busch) Series event. We were racing down Daytona International Speedway's long, flat backstretch when Buckshot Jones got into Dick Trickle, who got into me and sent me into a spin. My Chevy turned backward, took off like an airplane wing, and did a complete barrel roll midair. The right side of my car landed squarely on Trickle's hood, which tipped me over and slammed the left front corner of the car hard into the infield grass. It hit so violently the car bounced back up into the air and did a 360-degree turn through the grass before I finally bumped up against the big concrete wall in the infield and came to a stop.

After I got checked out in the infield care center, I walked out to chat with the media folks who had gathered outside, like they always do. I told CBS Sports that I was "just a little bit woozy." Then I turned to talk to a group of sportswriters. As I began to describe the flip, I actually fell backward—like nearly fainted—and had to be caught before I flopped onto the ground. I laughed about it, and so did the reporters I was talking to. When I went to the race shop that week we were laughing again when the guys on the crew showed me the inside of the car. When my car had slammed down on the ground, it caused my head to hit the roll cage so hard that my helmet had put a big dent into the bar. A steel bar. There was a mark on the top left corner of my helmet that matched that dent perfectly.

That same day I was up inside the car, lying on my back on the floorboard doing some electrical work under the dash, and the strangest thing happened. Suddenly, I felt like the car was being rolled across the floor of the shop with me in it. I sat up and realized it hadn't moved an inch. I shook my head, rubbed my eyes, thought, *Whoa, that was weird*, and went back to work.

So, after hitting my head so hard that it bent steel, had me sounding totally groggy on national television, dang near caused me to pass out in the middle of a conversation, and made a car I was working on feel like it had zipped across the room, what was my treatment of choice? To go home, lay on the couch, and put a washcloth on my head.

Ol' Hammerhead, right?

Four years later, in 2002, auto racing was in the middle of a total safety overhaul. NASCAR, IndyCar, Formula One, you name it—everyone was implementing all sorts of changes, all of them overdue. Racetracks started lining their retaining walls with "soft wall" barriers, sanctioning bodies mandated the use of head and neck restraints, and drivers started changing how they built their seats and, really, how everything was situated around them inside the car. Why? Because of a stretch of terrible deaths. But really, what had finally spurred it all was the death of my father at the end of the 2001 Daytona 500. Entering the final turn of the race his car was turned into the wall, and he was killed by the blunt force of his car's right front corner impacting the bare concrete wall. Other drivers had died from the same injury, but this was different. If the Intimidator, the toughest man alive, could be killed, then everyone was vulnerable. Overnight every racer was either buying or inventing gear they hoped would help them avoid what had happened to my dad and all those who'd died before him. It was a lot of big changes all at once.

What didn't change was the racers' mentality of toughing it out and walking it off. It was still considered the worst thing for a driver to be perceived in the garage as damaged goods. That's why, in 2002, I chose to tell no one about what had happened to me in the season's tenth race, a 500-miler at the big, sweeping two-mile California Speedway in Fontana, California, just one week after I had taken my second consecutive win at Talladega.

Anyone watching that day knew that I had taken a huge shot late in the race. Kevin Harvick, driving my father's old ride, was cutting down toward the entrance to pit road and stuffed the nose of his Chevy into the passenger's side door of mine. I got turned toward the Turn 4 wall and slid into it so hard that it bent the entire left front of the car, so deep it looked like that whole corner had been sawed off. The hood was bowed to the point that it stuck several feet up into the air. There's no doubt that the newly redesigned interior of the car, the new seat, and the head and neck restraint I was wearing—all implemented after my father's death—kept me from getting hurt way worse than I was. But my head was ringing, a dull sensation inside my skull. The breath had been knocked out of me, my body was sore, and I thought I might've been hurt bad.

If you look at the video now, you can see plain as day that right there, just seconds after the crash, I was already worried about looking like I was hurt. I didn't want anyone to see if I was, so I basically ran past the medical team and jumped into the ambulance. On the telecast, analyst Darrell Waltrip said a couple of times that he thought I'd just had the breath knocked out of me. That was good. That's what I wanted people to think. But it was wrong. I had suffered a concussion. Unlike Daytona in 1998, I knew this one was no joke. But I kept it to myself, even when the symptoms didn't subside over the next few weeks.

I was twenty-seven and a pretty hard partier in those days, so I think most people figured that if I was dragging or looking tired, I'd been up drinking beers all night. A lot of times, I probably had, but not now. I just felt like I had. For at least a month I felt like I'd had a couple of beers all the time, morning, noon, night, and even when I was behind the wheel of my racecar. During that stretch, we ran terrible. In fact, we ran awful all summer long. Meanwhile, I managed to keep my secret all the way until the end of September. By then I was feeling fine and we were running near the front again, so in an interview leading up to the race at the year-old Kansas Speedway, I confessed that I had run several races during spring and summer while I was—and this is exactly how I put it—"feeling a little loopy."

NASCAR was not happy about that confession. It dominated the headlines all weekend. But I certainly wasn't alone. Other drivers and former drivers backed me up by adding their own stories of hiding concussions over the years. The most notable was Dale Jarrett, a series champion, future NASCAR Hall of Famer, and someone whose opinion has always been deeply respected throughout the sport. He admitted that he had no recollection of the inaugural Kansas Speedway event one year earlier, thanks to a concussion suffered in the closing laps of the race. None. His memory had been erased to the point that he said when he came back for that 2002 race people had to show him where the garage and driver motorcoach lot were. It was like he'd never been there before.

In the middle of all that public confessing, NASCAR announced changes to how drivers would be evaluated after hard hits like mine. Until then, if the doctor who did the initial, quick examination in the infield care center cleared that driver to leave without admitting him to a hospital, then NASCAR assumed that meant he was good to go and cleared to drive, physically and mentally. Those infield checkups were the same as they'd basically always been: pretty simple. Everyone has fibbed to their doctor from time to time during a routine physical, right? He says, "How have you been feeling?" and we say, "Oh, I'm fine," just to get out of there and go home. Racecar drivers didn't just do that from time to time. They did that all the time. Most probably still do. Why? I said it to those reporters in 2002 and it's still true: I didn't want to tell anyone how bad I'd felt until after I got better and I started running better because I didn't want anyone to think I was broken, that I was messed up.

I had seen drivers get hurt before, and I had heard how people talked about them behind their backs. I love the people in the NASCAR garage and I know a lot of them love me, but they will cut you from the herd if they think you're going to slow them down. It had just happened with my teammate Steve Park the year before. He suffered a head injury in a freak accident at Darlington Raceway and had worked his butt off to come back. Yet when he didn't immediately start running up front like he was doing before the crash, all I heard was, "Well, there you go. Steve was awesome, but you know what? He'll never be the same again."

There was no way I was putting myself in that situation. I had worked so hard to prove I belonged at NASCAR's highest level because of my ability, not just because of my name. There was no way I was going to start back at zero with everyone. In my mind, if I had fessed up about my concussion that summer, when we were running twenty-to-thirty-something-place every weekend, then my career and my image might not ever recover. "Ol' Junior, he's finished. Just like Steve Park. He'll never be the same again." That's why I waited. It's no coincidence that I chose to finally admit it all after we'd picked up a few top-ten finishes over the month and a half leading into that Kansas race.

The morning of that race, NASCAR announced on national television that they were changing their policies and would now be watching drivers much more closely during those post-crash exams. If the infield doctor had even the smallest bit of worry that there might have been a concussion, then he was supposed to immediately call for further scans and tests.

Every race day begins with what we call a drivers' meeting,

when every driver, crew chief, team owner, and NASCAR official goes over the ground rules for that day's event. It's part of our routine. But when this meeting ended and I went to leave like I always did, NASCAR president Mike Helton told me to sit back down. I've known Mike nearly my whole life. He's one of my father figures. In that moment he talked to me like a father figure, in his always-calm, sorta-quiet but still sorta-scary tone of his. He told me he wasn't happy. He told me about the policy changes. And he told me to never do that again, racing when I didn't feel right or kind of shrug it off publicly like I had that week. This was serious business, and he wanted me to treat it as such.

So what did I do? I joked about it on national television. An hour later, during the pre-race TV coverage, NBC Sports ran a whole segment on the mess, showing my California crash and interviewing Mike Helton about how mad he was. It even included an interview with driver Jeff Burton, now my coworker at NBC, in which he admitted how easy it was for drivers to fake their way through post-crash exams and said that everyone did it. Then they came to me for a live interview.

"Dale, do you feel like you put your fellow competitors in any danger by racing with a concussion after your wreck at California?"

"Nah, not really. I mean, even at 80 percent I'm still better than probably half those guys out there . . ."

I was joking. I guess I was trying to sound like my dad. Then I went to explain myself.

"I thought about that, but it was a situation where I made my own decision. I would've accepted the repercussions from that no matter what they were . . ." I admitted that I handled it wrong, that I'd hurt the trust between myself and NASCAR a little, and said that I felt like being out on the track was the best way for me to evaluate exactly how bad of shape I was really in. I told everyone that I'd kept to myself because I didn't want to cause any alarm, because, hey, it wasn't as serious as everyone was making it out to be.

But what was my biggest regret at the time, so much so I said it twice? That the concussion had been just enough to keep us from competing for the Winston Cup championship at year's end.

Today, when I go back and watch that interview, I don't laugh at that 80 percent comment like I used to. When I watch that roll cage–denting 1998 Daytona 300 wreck on YouTube, I don't laugh at that anymore either. I have the same feeling whenever I watch other old races and see crashes like the one at Daytona in '84 that caused Ricky Rudd to have to tape his eyelids open. I used to watch that stuff and see pure awesomeness. Action and danger and thrills and a fearless racer doing his thing.

You know what I see now? I see Ricky Rudd's head in the car. I see how much it travels around in the cockpit, being thrown around and bouncing off of stuff. I think about those taped-open eyelids and, yeah, it's a cool story to tell, but it was probably just scratching the surface of what all had actually happened to Ricky inside his head . . . or to my father when he had a hard crash . . . or to me, when I see myself so desperate to get into that ambulance at Fontana before anyone could judge me . . . or to any driver who came up racing in the world that we all did.

I told you, I love racing. That will never change. But the way I look at racing has changed. Really, the way I look at the whole world has changed. Why? What happened to make me feel that way? It all goes back to what was supposed to be a run-of-the-mill Wednesday afternoon in Kansas City, back at the same track where ten years earlier I'd caused such a controversy.

CHAPTER 2

INTO THE FOG

Wednesday, August 29, 2012
Kansas Speedway

I've never been a big fan of tire tests. You can probably attribute that to my DNA. My father was notorious for finding substitute drivers to sit in for him during tests. In racing, midweek test sessions are a necessary evil. We run lap after lap as fast as we can go, finding the limits of what will and won't work on a racecar when we come back to that track with trophies on the line. Those test laps are when crew chiefs, engineers, auto manufacturers, tire makers, even the folks who run the racetracks all gather data and information to see what works and what doesn't. That goes for drivers, too, but really our job is to run the car as hard as it will go, give them as much data as possible, and then let the others take that information and see what they can do with it.

But it can get boring—a day of running laps all by yourself, stopping only to pull into the garage and sit there while the engineers run their tests. If you follow me on social media, then you know I'm kind of addicted to my phone. On these days I keep it in the car to give me something to do between runs. I'm always checking social media, texting Amy, whatever.

This particular Wednesday was for me the tensest kind of test—a tire test. Goodyear is NASCAR's exclusive tire supplier, and they provide different types of tires to teams depending on what type of track we're running, whether it's a big superspeedway like Daytona and Talladega, a short track like Richmond and Martinsville, or one of our bread-and-butter intermediate tracks, like the one-and-a-half-mile Kansas Speedway. When Goodyear has a tire compound they feel they need to run through its paces or if there's been a significant change to a racetrack and they want to make sure they are ready for it, then they will book a test session with a team or several teams to serve as their guinea pigs for the day.

In this case they needed to take a look at both the tire and the track. They had a tire that had been having some issues on intermediate tracks, and the place where we were on this day, Kansas Speedway, had just been repaved. When I say a tire test is tense, it's because of what the mission of that test really is. If they ask you to do it, you always say yes because it's good for any race team to get in any extra practice laps whenever they can. But it's tense because what Goodyear really wants to see is where the limit is, how far their tire can go. The trick for the driver is to find that edge and ride right on it without pushing too far and going over it.

Whenever a racetrack gets new blacktop it is super fast. We'd been at Kansas Speedway for two days, and we were flying around the track. There were a handful of cars there, and we were all quick, but I was the fastest car there, and everyone knew it.

It wasn't just this test. We had been fast all season long. I was in my second season with Steve Letarte as my crew chief, and we were in the groove, man. We started the year finishing second in the Daytona 500 and had never slowed down. We won at Michigan on June 17, snapping a nearly four-year losing streak, and spent all summer ranked either first or second in the championship standings. This was the best I had raced and the best I had felt in a long time.

I was starting the final lap of a 25-lap run and had really picked up the pace. I was coming down the frontstretch, and I was in the gas, big time. I had just topped out at 205 mph as the car entered the bottom of Turn 1. Just as I lifted out of the gas at the entrance of the turn, my right front tire popped. Just, *BOOM*. A tremendous amount of heat had built up within the tread pattern of the tire as it grabbed that new asphalt. The joint where the sidewall of the tire meets the tread had gotten to the point where it just couldn't take the heat any longer. I mean, it just exploded. A whole chunk of the sidewall, big as a couple of fists, blew off.

With nothing to hold the leading edge of the car to the racetrack, there was no way for me to steer it. My Chevy took a hard righthand turn and shot directly up the 17-degree banking, like a ramp, into the outside retaining wall. I was traveling at about 185 mph when I hit that wall.

It was a nightmare blast of a hit. I've raced from the time I was a teenager, into nearly my mid-forties, and nothing has ever come anywhere close to how nasty that hit was. NASCAR installs Incident Data Recorders—or, as we call them, "black boxes"—that are similar to the crash data recorders that are used in airplanes. They can measure the acceleration and deceleration of our racecars 10,000 times per second. That information is used to figure out how much force was exerted during a crash, measured in Gs. They were mandated in 2002, another part of all the safety innovations that took place after my dad's death the year before. Today's more advanced measurements are even better (and the black boxes are actually blue now). As digital technology has improved, so has the ability to record and gather data.

My hit at Kansas registered at 40 Gs. That's a lot. Anything over 25 or 30 is considered big, and this was way over that. Honestly, it felt like more.

The impact was so loud that my friend and fellow racer Brad Keselowski, who was also participating in the tire test, said he heard the impact in the garage, nearly half a mile away. It was so violent that Steve Letarte, who saw it from the roof of our team's transporter truck, didn't even wait for the rescue crew to get out there to me, stunned and trying to climb out of my destroyed car. Stevie immediately scrambled down off the hauler, ran to his rental car, and drove all the way out into the turn himself to check on me.

Brad did the same. When Brad heard what he said "sounded like a plane crash," he ran to where he could see the turn where I'd hit. What he saw was the tell-tale black marks on the asphalt that traced my path from the spot where the tire had blown to where my car was now, still stuck in the fence at the top of the banking. That's what worried Brad: my car hadn't bounced off the wall and slid back down the banking but was still jammed up there in the steel and foam of the "soft wall" barrier. The nose of my Chevy was stuck in there like a dart. It also bothered him that he kept watching for several minutes and a safety crew had yet to arrive, so, like Steve, he jumped into his rental car and hustled out there.

It looked bad. I knew it had been a vicious hit. But at the time

I didn't think anything was unusually wrong with me physically. Whenever you crash, you kind of do a personal systems check. Anything feel broken? Everything moving and working okay?

I did that check and climbed out of the car. When Brad and Steve got to me, I was leaning up against the wall, still catching my breath. There was still no ambulance, only a tow truck, and it had arrived at the same time as Brad in his rental car. He gave me a lift back to the garage and asked me if I was okay. When I didn't respond, he didn't think much of it. We're good friends. Brad used to drive for me and even used to live in a house on my property. He's always described me as "a man of few words." So my giving him a couple of one-word answers to his questions about the crash and the tire failure—that was nothing out of the ordinary.

When he dropped me off at our hauler in the garage, the team was already preparing to unload the backup car and get me back out there. I asked how long it would be before that car was ready. Just put a washcloth on it, right? Walk it off.

But Steve said the car wouldn't *be* ready. He'd made that decision the instant I hit the wall. We were done. There was no way he was going to put me back on the track in another car. He'd seen the hit. He'd seen me. He was just spooked enough that he was like, nope, our day is over.

I felt like I was going to be sore but, other than that, okay. But standing there in the Kansas Speedway garage, one of my crew guys, Jason Burdett, who has also been a friend of mine forever, was staring at me, watching me, like he was doing a Dale Jr. systems check. I asked him what was up, and he said, "Something ain't right with you. Just the way you're looking. The way you're looking at me right now, the way you're looking around, you just look messed up. You look glassed over, weird looking."

I laughed it off, but now, a few minutes after the crash, I started to realize that Jason wasn't wrong. Something wasn't right.

I went with the team to a barbecue joint across the street from the track. My plane had come to Kansas City from North Carolina with Amy and my buddy Sawmill Hoover onboard. As soon as we were done eating I was going to jet off with them to DC to see the Washington Redskins play a preseason game against Tampa Bay. But, like Jason, anyone who really knew me and was closely watching me knew something was wrong. Like Brad says, I'm kind of a quiet guy anyway, especially in groups, so it's not unusual for me not to say a lot in a situation like that where a bunch of us are eating together. But this was different. Steve said later that he had immediately noticed I was even more reserved than usual.

He was right. My head was raging. I was starting to feel worse, like everything was moving away from me, kind of like that time I was working under my car in 1998 and it felt like it had suddenly moved across the room. Only this was worse. I was there with them in that restaurant, but really, I wasn't. The best way I know to describe it is *unplugged*.

I remember all of it, the whole day. I remember the moments before the Kansas crash, the crash itself, and everything about Steve and lunch. But all of that happened in a state of shellshock. Sure, I had been "woozy" that day at Daytona in '98, and I'd had that mess in 2002. This feeling though, this was different.

I use that word, *shellshock*, because I think about the depictions we've seen in war movies, when a soldier has an explosion happen right next to him and—*boom*—he's just in a daze. That's it. That's the feeling. You see fine, but your eyes aren't really focused on anything. You hear what's going on just fine too. There's no ringing in your ears or anything like that, but it's like everyone and all activity around you is a thousand feet away. You know what's happening, and you know that it's right there in front of you, but it feels detached. It's like you're not actually there. It's more like you're watching a scene in a movie that you're in. You know what the people you are with are talking about, but if they turned to you and said, "Hey, Dale, what do you think about that?" the only response your mind can come up with is going to be, "I don't even understand what you're talking about right now." It's like you understand the words of the language being spoken, but you don't actually know what those words even mean.

You might find that description confusing, even frustrating. Now imagine that feeling in your head. All the time. And it just won't straighten out or quiet down. That's where I was.

While we were waiting on our food, I was watching everyone from the team, probably a dozen people having six different conversations, and I was overcome with a massive wave of nausea like I'd never had before. If I could have I would have laid down right in the middle of the floor of that restaurant. I couldn't do that, so my next instinct was to just jump up and run out of there, but I didn't want to freak everyone out, and I sure didn't want to throw up all over everyone. So I tried to calmly excuse myself, like I was just walking outside to take a phone call. But I was freaking out. My pulse was racing, and I know I was as white as a sheet.

I must have looked pretty bad because I remember the other people in the restaurant and the waiters and waitresses all looking at me like, "Hey, look, there's Junior! Man, what's up with him? He looks messed up."

I got outside and just as I did a limousine pulled up. It was Amy and Sawmill, coming to meet up with me to fly to the Redskins game. Thank God. I climbed into that limo and immediately laid down on the floor, flat on my back. The only thing that made me feel even the slightest bit better was to be horizontal.

Amy was scared. I was scared. She saw the same glassed-over look in my eyes that Jason and Steve had seen. But when she asked me if I was okay, I just told her I'd be fine. We actually went back inside and ate. Then we went to the game. My feeling of being detached continued the whole time, even when I made a TV appearance later that night in the ESPN broadcast booth. I'm such a huge Redskins fan, and I've always prided myself on knowing everything there is to know about the team, but I was concentrating so hard just to make sure I made any sense during that interview that I probably made things worse in my head.

I'd called the level of confusion I was experiencing after Kansas "woozy." This was way more than woozy. But I still did what I'd always done—the same thing I'd done with Amy in the limo and to the whole world in 2002. I just pushed through it that night. I went home and went to bed, figuring that this time would be like those other times. I would sleep it off. And on Thursday morning, certainly by the time we hit the race weekend at Atlanta, I would feel fine.

That's how it worked, right? It always cleared up, eventually. Put a washcloth on it.

The next morning, the fog was still there. The detachment was still there. I was nauseous all the time. I waited for it to go away, but when I woke up Friday it was still the same. That morning, as Steve was driving into the tunnel to enter Atlanta Motor Speedway with the team, I called him and told him that I wasn't sure I was going to be able to race that weekend. This was just a few hours before practice was scheduled to begin!

Steve knew this decision was above his pay grade, so he called our boss, team owner Rick Hendrick, and they decided that if I wasn't up to it, then we just wouldn't race that weekend. No substitute driver. We were having a great season. We'd already won a race and were locked into the postseason, so we wouldn't risk it if I didn't want to.

So what did I do? I showed up and raced. We were bad slow in practice and qualifying all weekend and started Sunday night's 500-mile race thirty-fifth out of forty-three cars. But it's a long race, and Steve got the car dialed in late. I made a run up into the top ten, and we finished seventh. Less than a week later, I won the pole position at Richmond and led 67 laps. Then we finished eighth at Chicagoland Speedway . . . thirteenth the next week . . . eleventh the next . . . We weren't running as well as we had during the summer, but we were rolling along. Our postseason—the Chase—had started, and we were still among the top championship contenders, ranked seventh in the standings with seven races remaining.

Throughout all of these races, though, I still felt sick, detached, and nauseous. A lot. It went on for a month after the Kansas crash, but again, I didn't tell anyone. Once the initial glassy-eyed look went away, I could even downplay it to Amy. I had dull headaches, but the real frustration was I felt like my mind was lagging a little. I might have a hard time finding a word to describe something, or my eyes might track something, but my head felt like it was behind it, swishy, again like I'd had a few beers.

What I did was make an adjustment like I would with a racecar that wasn't handling quite right. I figured out how to live with it, how to fake my way through it, and how to work around it so that people around me couldn't see how bad I really felt. Besides, we were running pretty well, and any time I was at the racetrack I was able to keep my mind off of my symptoms. At home, I might've spent my time thinking about how I felt, but I found that at the track, when I was focused on the car, all I thought about was racing. As a result my symptoms weren't really an issue. By the time we got to Talladega, six weeks after my Kansas crash, honestly, I felt awesome. Just like those other times—in 1998 or 2002, you name it—the fog was lifting.

Then it wasn't.

Sunday, October 7, 2012
Talladega Superspeedway

We were coming through the final two turns of the final lap of the day, and the field at Talladega was just a gigantic traffic jam. There were twenty-eight cars in the lead pack, including a wad of sixteen of us running in four rows, lined up four-wide. I had just moved up to sit right smack in the middle of the first row of that group, running tenth with the leaders in my sight, directly in front of me. I knew the chances of a Big One were high, as in, it was almost definitely going to happen. Maybe I could take advantage and pick up a bunch of spots in a hurry.

Sure enough, it did. Tony Stewart was leading and defending his position, as he should have been with twenty-seven of us in his rearview mirror. Michael Waltrip snuck underneath Tony at the bottom of Turn 3, and they made contact. It started a chain reaction that would end up wrecking twenty-five cars. Twenty-five! That is as big of a Big One as you'll ever see. Tony got sideways, fell out of the lead, and slid helplessly up into our pack. He was hit simultaneously by two oncoming cars and flipped into the air. The two cars that hit him were the ones I'd been running door-to-door with. He sailed by me as I started braking to keep from hitting anyone too hard as cars were out of control and all over the place right in front of me. As we all kept sliding and other cars kept smashing into each other, my Chevy actually sliced through a hole in the middle of it all and, though I was pointed in the wrong direction—downward toward the infield—I was in the clear. For a second, anyway.

When you're in the Big One, you're just like a boat stuck in a storm. You can react and steer and dig all you want, but really, you're just praying for the best. You have little or no control. It's just screeches and smoke and chaos. What you don't want to hear is that crunch, that smack that tells you that you've been hit. It's so incredibly jarring, not just physically, but mentally, even when you've braced yourself. So as I was sliding along there, falling out of the turn toward the infield, my mind was like, *Oh, man . . . don't hit anything . . . don't hit anything . . .* Then, when my car got out in the open and slowly headed down the banking toward the grass with all that happening behind me way up at the wall, it got kind of quiet around me. That was good. My thoughts turned a little more positive, into *Okay, we're good? Are we? Yeah, we're good!*

The nose of my car had just touched the safety of the grass—and I was doored.

Bobby Labonte had driven way down onto the apron at the bottom of the banking to avoid all the crashing. Problem was, Brad Keselowski had done the same. When Brad saw me coming down the track and moved to avoid me, he turned in front of Bobby, who bounced off Brad and directly into me. He hit my car just behind the driver's side door area. It helicoptered me. I spun around twice, all the way off the turn and onto the frontstretch. There, just when I was starting to slow down, I was hit in the left rear quarter panel by another wrecked car—Tony Stewart, still helplessly wrecking along, half a mile away from where he'd first gotten airborne—and I was sent into one more 360-degree spin, this one nearly as jarring as the first.

I had suffered another concussion. I knew it. I knew it instantly. And I was instantly scared to death. Were you kidding me? Two more concussions? In six weeks? That shellshock like I'd experienced at Kansas returned in a snap. At the same time, it felt different. This time, there would be no hiding anything from anyone because something had happened that took away my ability to do my usual "Naw, man, I'm cool" thing. Whatever had happened to me at Talladega had instantly taken away my ability to control my emotions. Now I was just angry. Angry all the time. I drove my wrecked car back to the garage, and ESPN had a TV camera there waiting on me, part of a big pack of reporters waiting to ask me about the crash. I started talking and my eyes got wide and my volume picked up and my face started turning red.

"I can't believe that everybody, that nobody's sensible enough to realize how ridiculous that was . . . I mean, that was ridiculous! If this is what we do every week I won't be doing it, I'll just put it to you like that. If this is how we race every week I'll find another job. It's bloodthirsty. If that's what people want, that's ridiculous. I don't even want to go to Daytona or Talladega next year. But I ain't got much choice . . . If this is how we're gonna race, and that's how we're gonna continue to race and nothing's gonna change, I think NASCAR should build the cars. It'd save us a lot of money."

Bloodthirsty? NASCAR should build the cars? I don't want to race at Daytona or Talladega? Does any of that sound like me? Not a chance. But something had been triggered. It had been broken. All of a sudden I had this anger, this rage inside of me that I couldn't control. And there was nothing working properly inside my head that would have stopped me from just throwing that rage right out there for everyone to see and hear it.

The aftershocks from Kansas had taken a while to set in. But here at Talladega, as I talked to the media, the inside of my head felt like there was a huge amount of physical pressure. It felt like my head was filling up with blood. I was so scared that I had given myself some sort of real physical injury, like I had bleeding on the brain. I remember riding out of the racetrack on a golf cart, headed to the air strip behind the track, and just trying so hard for the people with me to not see that I was totally flipping out. All I could think about was, *Man, here we go again.* It took a month for those feelings from Kansas to go away and now it was all back again? And it felt worse? So how long was it going to take for this to go away? I knew it already felt worse than Kansas, at least here in the first few minutes following the crash, so what did that mean? I'd had two concussions now, back to back, so was this going to be worse because of that? Had I just ripped the scab off my brain just as it was almost healed?

That night at my house was my thirty-eighth birthday party. Honestly, I don't remember a ton about it. I was too preoccupied, too worried. Brad Keselowski was there and had brought a bunch of fireworks. Like, big fireworks. He says he noticed that as they were setting them off, I was just sitting by the campfire, kind of staying off to myself. My not having much to say at Kansas six weeks earlier—he hadn't thought much about that. But this struck him as odd.

That night, I did something I should have done a lot earlier. I told Amy everything. I told her how awful I felt and how I had lost my emotional control. I told her that while she knew I'd been dinged up at Kansas and how badly I'd felt initially, she never really knew the full extent of how I was feeling because I didn't let her know.

She certainly didn't know that the concussion symptoms had gone on for more than a month. No one had known but me. That had to change, and I was ending the silence right then and there before I let the secrecy go too far.

It was such a relief to finally say those things out loud. But it was hard. What we agreed to do the next day was going to be even harder.

Monday, October 8, 2012

The next morning Amy and I drove over to the headquarters of my race team, JR Motorsports. You need to understand something about JRM. That place is way more than just your regular NASCAR race shop. It's the headquarters of all my businesses, from Hammerhead Entertainment to the Dale Jr. Foundation. It's also my extended family. We have nearly 150 employees, and several of those folks are members of my actual family.

That starts with my sister, Kelley Earnhardt Miller. Her official title is co-owner/vice president/business manager. In other words, she's the boss. Years ago, she took a pay cut to come run my businesses, but she did it because looking after her little brother has been her job ever since I arrived in this world two years after she did.

Our childhood wasn't easy. Our parents split up when we were kids. We went with our mother, Brenda, and we moved from house to house. After one of our homes burned up in a fire, we moved in with my dad and his wife, Teresa, just as he was becoming a NASCAR superstar. That meant he was gone a lot. And that meant Kelley was the one who was raising me. At one point I was sent to military school—you know, I guess to undo some of that

Hammerheadedness—and Kelley quit her school and enrolled in the military school that I'd been sent off to, just to look out for me. That's how awesome my sister is.

That's who Amy and I went to see the Monday morning after the restless night that followed Talladega. I told Kelley how bad I was feeling and how the wreck less than twenty-four hours ago had caused that. Then I told her how I'd hidden my concussion from Kansas and how it had just now gotten better, but now it was back again and I was in bad shape. We called my big boss, Rick Hendrick, the owner of my Cup Series ride, and told him what I'd just told Kelley. Rick insisted that I go see Dr. Jerry Petty and that I do it immediately.

In the motorsports world, especially in the NASCAR world, there is no more respected or trusted doctor—I would even go so far as to say no more respected person—than Dr. Jerry Petty. He is not related to Richard Petty, but among people who make their living in the NASCAR business, he is looked at with the same respect and regard as the King. He's a neurologist who has worked on international motorsports councils, been a team doctor for the Carolina Panthers, and served as neurological consultant to the NFL and the NFL Players Association.

But he's also a natural-born member of the NASCAR community. He's from Gastonia, North Carolina, just outside of Charlotte. He went to school at UNC–Chapel Hill and started working races at Charlotte Motor Speedway's infield care center in 1970. Dr. Petty was one of the key figures in helping NASCAR through its massive safety changes after my dad was killed in 2001. Five years later he won the Bill France NASCAR Award of Excellence, an honor that goes to people who have reached the top level of lifetime achievements in motorsports. In other words, if Dr. Petty tells you something, no one in the NASCAR garage argues with him. He's earned that honor a thousand times over.

My entire life he has been the guy that racecar drivers want to see when they are facing the scariest moments of their lives, the first moments after they've been badly injured in a crash on the racetrack, or like me on this day in 2012 and in the days following. No one likes feeling vulnerable, but racecar drivers hate it more than maybe anyone else in the world. So, in that moment, they want to see someone they can trust. A good doctor is no different than a good crew chief. When they tell you what's wrong and they tell you how to go about fixing what's wrong, you don't question them because their record tells you they know what they are doing. You trust them. Everyone trusts Dr. Petty.

Tuesday, October 9, 2012

When Amy and I arrived at his office in Charlotte, Dr. Petty took me in his office and gave me an ImPACT test. That stands for Immediate Post-Concussion Assessment and Cognitive Testing. It's actually pretty simple, but don't mistake simple for easy.

The ImPACT really starts as an interview, getting your medical history and asking a series of questions to help figure out how a patient really feels. It goes through twenty-plus concussion symptoms. Am I dizzy? Am I nauseous? Do I have headaches and if so, what are they like? Then there are a series of tests to measure how fast or slow the brain is processing different kinds of information. Visual memory, verbal memory, reaction time, visual motor speed. You sit in front of a computer terminal for twenty to thirty minutes and it throws a bunch of fast-moving exams at you. It gives you a dozen words to memorize, but only flashes them up there quick, twice. Then they double up, adding another dozen to the first ones you saw, but you're still only supposed to remember the first ones, the target words. Say you might get *car* in the first group and *truck* in the second. Then later a window pops up and says, "Was *car* one of the words displayed?" There are similar drills using shapes, letters, colors, stuff like that. It's a lot to process all at once, and that's how it's designed. The idea is to push your brain, put it to work, and see where its limits are.

I had already done this test with Dr. Petty once before. We did that to give him a baseline to work from should we ever find ourselves in the situation I was in now. In fact, the reason that NASCAR would mandate baseline ImPACT testing in 2014 was in no small part because of what I was about to go through now, in 2012.

Before that, doctors just eyeballed it. The idea was, *Well, hey, this doctor knows this guy, so he'll know if something's wrong as soon as he sees him!* But thankfully, that's changed. Some racers had complained about talk of a NASCAR mandate for baseline testing—being "forced" to take an ImPACT test—but I can promise you that anyone who found themselves in my situation would've stopped complaining. IndyCar had already been doing baseline testing for a while, and now I knew how valuable that was. Because I had taken the test before my concussions, Dr. Petty had real data to use as a measuring stick. What was I capable of when I was healthy, and what was I capable of now? He took the results of my test on this day and compared them to the test I'd taken before either one of my big 2012 hits.

It wasn't awful, but it wasn't great, either. My memory was dragging in spots where it hadn't before. So was my reaction time. Not a lot, but there was definitely a difference. Dr. Petty told me that just by looking at the comparison between those test scores he knew I had suffered a concussion. When that was added to my stories of what had happened at both Kansas and Talladega, there was no question that I had an issue that needed to be treated.

He called for a detailed MRI scan the next morning. The scan is used to find real, physical damage and uses a special method that can also sift through any damage done from previous injuries. Those scans looked good and also ruled out any other causes, such as tumors. The fact that I had suffered no amnesia on either side of either accident was also good news.

Wednesday, October 10, 2012

Dr. Petty says that the night before the MRI, he sat up going over the math problem in his head: my ImPACT scores + my personal recollection of both crashes + his personal observances of me. It was up to him to clear me to drive or tell me to sit. But even before the MRI came back normal on Wednesday, he'd already made his decision. He'd called Rick that morning. Then he and Rick met with Kelley, Steve, Amy, and others. They all called me into a room, sat me down, and told me that they didn't believe I needed to be in my racecar at Charlotte that weekend.

When I describe it here, it sounds like an intervention, doesn't it? But that's not what it was. Amy had the best description of it. She called it an emotional support group. They explained to me that they weren't forcing me to do something; instead they were telling me they were worried about me and that's why they thought this was the best thing for me to do.

They were afraid of how I would react because I'm a racer, and they were right to be worried. As I've already told you, racers don't get out of their racecars. In a dozen seasons at NASCAR's top level

I had never missed a start. My streak was up to 461 races. Now that was going to end.

I was shocked. We were still in the NASCAR Chase for the Championship. After my Talladega crash, we were no longer one of the favorites, but we were still fighting. Not only that, the Charlotte race weekend was scheduled to start the very next day, with qualifying on Thursday night. But when I looked around that room I realized that there wasn't a single person in there who didn't care about me. They also all depended on me to help them make their livings. So no one in there was ever going to make me miss a race unless they truly believed that it was the absolute right thing to do.

Though I don't think I realized it at the time, I know now that deep down I was also a little relieved. My secret was out there. We had identified a problem. We were gonna fix it.

Rick and Steve went about finding a driver for my racecar for Charlotte, thankfully taking my suggestion and hiring my friend Regan Smith, a guy who needed a lucky break. Kelley and the folks at Hendrick Motorsports went about planning a press conference for the next day, when I would reveal to the world that I would be getting out of my car in the middle of the postseason not only because of a concussion suffered at Talladega but also because of a concussion suffered at Kansas that I had kept hidden.

Thursday, October 11, 2012
Charlotte Motor Speedway

I don't remember being nervous about the press conference. Again, I think I was more relieved to get it out there and not have to pretend any longer, and I was also anxious to get on with whatever was next, to get healed up and get back into my racecar.

It was me, Steve, Rick, and Dr. Petty sitting at the front of the Charlotte Motor Speedway media center. The reaction to what we said, after the initial shock wore off that I was going to sit out two races, was overwhelmingly positive. The media wrote that I was open and honest, and they suggested that maybe I had helped start an important discussion in the garage about a very important topic that had always been an uncomfortable conversation. There was still that part of me that sat there and worried about being viewed as damaged goods by my fellow racers. On the microphone, live on national TV, I told everyone that I felt 100 percent and that sitting wasn't what I wanted to do, but what I had been told to do, and I wasn't going to argue with the doctors.

"I don't have any plans of being here this weekend," I said to the national media about the Charlotte race. "I think I'd be more of a distraction to the team and their efforts in the race. They've got a good opportunity to have a good run this weekend. And me staying away, to minimize that distraction, would help them out."

The truth was, I had somewhere else I had to be. Dr. Petty, Amy, and myself, we had a doctor's appointment. We were headed to Pittsburgh.

CHAPTER 3

BACK ON TRACK

Tuesday, October 16, 2012
Pittsburgh, Pennsylvania

When I stepped off the plane in Pittsburgh, I was stepping right into the center of the concussion world. This was ground zero for what had become the biggest controversy in sports: concussions and how they were affecting pro football players. It just so happened I was coming to town right when the fight between the NFL and its former players was getting pretty ugly, and as a result, a lot of the American public was really becoming aware of concussions for the first time.

It was a Pittsburgh Steeler, Pro Football Hall of Famer Mike Webster, who shook up the pro football world in 1999. He filed a disability claim that said his dementia had been caused by seventeen years of pounding to his head in the middle of the offensive line. He died on September 25, 2002—the exact same week that I'd gotten into so much hot water for confessing that I'd hidden my concussion earlier that season. It was a Pittsburgh-based medical examiner, Dr. Bennet Omalu, who did an examination of Webster's brain and became the first to discover that football players suffered from chronic traumatic encephalopathy, devastating microscopic trauma done by constant, repetitive damage. It causes systems failures in the brain and body. A lot of times the pain and the uncertainty of it all ended up driving victims into becoming people they'd never been before. At the time, no sports fan had any idea what that was. Now, every football fan knows the term CTE.

They certainly knew it by 2012. In April of that year, former NFL player Ray Easterling committed suicide, and an examination showed he suffered from CTE. Barely one month later, Junior Seau, one of the most popular NFL players of the 1990s, shot himself in the chest at the age of forty-three. Why in the chest? So that his brain would be intact and could be studied like Webster's.

The NFL was fighting to save its image, it was fighting with former players, and it was fighting with Dr. Omalu and others. That fight seemed to always come back to Pittsburgh. And now here I was, a racecar driver headed to see a doctor whose office was located, of all places, inside the Pittsburgh Steelers' training facility.

I wasn't sure how this was going to work. All I knew was that Dr. Jerry Petty had said this was where we had to go to receive the best diagnosis and treatment plan. He said, "You let Rick Hendrick and your sister worry about the racing stuff. We're going to see Micky" . . . and I didn't argue with him.

Micky is Dr. Michael Collins, founding member of the University of Pittsburgh Medical Center's Sports Medicine Concussion Program. He's known around the world for his expertise on sports-related concussions. He gives lectures, he teaches doctors and athletic trainers how to diagnose and treat concussions, and he works with the Steelers, Pittsburgh Penguins, Major League Baseball teams, even Cirque de Soleil. Remember that ImPACT test Dr. Petty used to identify my injuries? Well, Micky cofounded ImPACT.

That day, when I shook hands with him for the first time, I had no idea how much he would mean to my life, as a doctor but also as a friend. Micky has this real disarming way about him. You have to figure he's almost always the smartest guy in the room, right? On top of that, every conversation he has with a patient or a student is about the human brain, one of the most complicated, intimidating topics there is, period. And then, when he's meeting with his patients, you know that most of them are scared to death. Probably all of them. I know I was.

When we arrived at Micky's office, many patients were lined up. They were everything from professional athletes to kids who had been hurt playing youth sports to people who had been in car accidents on the street to construction workers who'd been hurt on the job. Looking around, in an instant, I learned two very important things. First, we were all in the same boat. We were all worried and confused and scared. Second, this Micky guy, he must be pretty dang good at what he does.

As soon as we sat down, he started handling me like a great crew chief would. We went over symptoms and how I was feeling, but I could tell he was already looking into me way deeper than that. He was evaluating me as a person. He immediately picked up on a couple of key pieces of my personality: that I can be a quiet guy and that I am also an information junkie. I can't learn or read enough about whatever it is that I'm thinking about at the time. I've always been that way. I guess it's me trying to keep up with my nonstop brain, trying to feed it. During the period of time when I'd kept my concussions to myself, I had been all over the internet, reading anything I could find, including all those stories about Mike Webster and Junior Seau and the others. I am also not the most patient person in the world. Stuff can't happen fast enough for me. That goes for anything, but especially when it comes to me and my racecar.

Micky sensed all of that about me very quickly. He says that only a few minutes into our first conversation in that examination room, he knew that (1) I'd had two injuries in a short period of time, the second coming while I was still experiencing the effects of the first; (2) after all my personal research, I was convinced that those concussions had been layered, repetitive injuries, not unlike what had caused CTE in those football players; (3) I wanted to get this over with as soon as possible; and (4) I was nervous that this was all ultimately headed toward someone like him telling me that my racing career was over.

With all of that in mind, the first thing Micky did was to start educating me. It was Brain Science 101. I would compare it to my explaining how a racecar works to someone who thinks they know but doesn't really know. He pulled out a sheet of paper, grabbed a pen, and sketched out a picture of a brain. He outlined for me how our brains operate.

Our brains are made up of billions of neurons that constantly process information and send out the signals that tell our bodies how to function and how to feel, physically and emotionally. Those neurons are connected by trillions of synapses, operating like a pipe or a fire hose, sending information like water up and down the line. We tend to think of it as this kind of mystical process, but it's actually pretty practical. It's amazing, but it ain't magic. It's physical and chemical. Brain activity is powered by electrical charges, sparked by the right combinations of positively and negatively charged chemicals, stuff like potassium and calcium—things we've all heard of. They keep information moving like a wave through those synapses and between those neurons and sending whatever it needs to on down the line through the rest of our body, reminding every organ and system how to do their jobs and waiting to help find solutions if any of those organs and systems run into problems.

All of that is happening within your brain, a three-pound organ that's basically the same consistency as a firm block of Jell-O. It seems very fragile when I describe it that way, and it is. So are all those cells doing all that communicating, especially those long, hose-like synapses. Our brains float along inside our skulls day and night, protected by cerebrospinal fluid and three layers of protective tissue called the meninges. Most of the time, that's enough to prevent injuries to your most important organ, even as fragile as it is. You're good.

Unless you hit a wall at 185 mph.

When our bodies experience giant collisions—really any big change in speed, like the deceleration of a racecar when it hits something—the brain can be jarred so hard against the inside of our skulls that there isn't much those layers of protection can do about it. Even if it doesn't hit anything, the shaking alone can be damaging. People hear the word *concussion* and they think about hits and impacts, but the roots of the word actually mean "to shake violently."

The brain is just like any other organ. It gets bruised. It bleeds. It swells. But even if none of that happens, those tiny little synapses can still get stretched, bent, or snapped, and the communication lines in your brain are interrupted. In other words, your body's information hose is stepped on. It gets holes and creases in it. The stuff that's supposed to stay out gets in, and the stuff that's supposed to be sent out gets stuck. The whole physical and chemical process is changed and, naturally, it stops working as well as it used to.

That's what Micky explained to me that day. That whole process, before and after injury. Then he explained that word—*injury*—and how it is never as simple as, "Well, patient, you have a concussion, so we're going to do this now . . ." because it's not a one-size-fits-all prognosis or treatment. He said something to me that day that I have remembered ever since and that I have repeated to anyone who will listen. He said, "Every concussion is like a snowflake. No two are alike." It makes sense when you really think about it. No two brains are alike; that's why no two people are alike, and that's why no two concussions are alike. Micky likes to say that there are about thirty different types of knee injuries, so why in the world would people assume that all brain injuries are the same?

And though no two concussions are exactly alike, that day he explained to me that they generally fall into six different types of brain injuries.

There's a *cognitive/fatigue concussion*, when patients experience a lag in their ability to concentrate. They get easily distracted, it's hard for them to retain information, and they get worn out way quicker as the day goes on.

There are *ocular concussions*, when your eyes can become disconnected, each eye kind of off doing its own thing, and you struggle trying to track something visually.

Post-traumatic migraine concussions are marked by headaches that just won't go away, often paired with becoming super sensitive to light and noise along with constant feelings of nausea.

Cervical concussions are injuries suffered farther down the neck and spine, also leading to constant migraines. When he told me about this one, I thought about all the racecar drivers I knew that I now figured had long suffered from these.

The description of *anxiety/mood concussions* felt familiar too. It's when the injured suddenly has a hard time turning off their thoughts and are constantly dogged by being stressed and worried all the time.

Finally, he said, he believed I was suffering from the sixth concussion type, known as a *vestibular concussion*. He said I had "decompensated my vestibular system." In other words, I had damaged the functioning ability of that system. The vestibular system is the balance center of your brain. That's where our minds interpret motion, stabilize our vision when we're moving, and coordinate the movements of our head and eyes. You know, pretty much everything you need to be a racecar driver.

He also explained that those six types are not mutually exclusive. You could suffer one type but the symptoms it causes could cross over into the symptoms of another type. Different sections of the brain control different types of thoughts and activities. If you suffered an injury to an area of the brain that works closely with another area, then both areas could be affected. The lines between concussions aren't black and white. Gray matter comes with a lot of gray areas.

I wanted to freak out. Deep down, I was. My feelings about the situation didn't improve when he explained to me that my spin at Talladega hadn't simply reaggravated the concussion from Kansas. This was a whole new injury. The Kansas hit was head-on, blunt-force to the front corner of my brain as it smacked the front of my skull. The Talladega accident had been a spin, like a centrifuge you see astronauts and fighter pilots training in, and it had whirled the back of my brain up against the back half of my skull. Micky said that I would have suffered the concussion at Talladega regardless, but that the first hit and the untreated injury I'd kept to myself had made me vulnerable. It made the second hit six weeks later much worse than it likely would've been on its own. Even more, my anxiety over it all—that self-inflicted stress I experienced between Kansas and Talladega, and in the days between Talladega and this appointment—had made things worse too. In the past, that connection wouldn't have been made. But now, Micky said, there was real evidence that anxiety accelerated injuries and symptoms.

So, yeah, freaking out, that's understandable, right? But while I remember everything that Micky said to me that day in the examination room, what Micky remembers is that I said nothing. He recalls that I looked nervous, anxious, worried, all the stuff you would expect from someone in that situation. But he also says now that he could tell I was internalizing a lot. He could tell that I wasn't completely showing my hand and that I was really good at that. I always have been. You figure out how to internalize your feelings when you grow up in the spotlight like I did, especially when you're trucking it through the world with the name Dale Earnhardt, and when there are hundreds of people who are depending on your name to make their living.

Not a lot of people pick that up about me, the internalizing. Certainly not during the first time they've ever met me. Micky did. He recognized it from his previous work with other high-profile athletes. That's how I knew Micky was someone to trust. He didn't just understand the science and the medicine of all this. He understood *me*.

And that's why I trusted him when he finished with his teaching session on brains and concussions and looked me right in the eye and said, "Dale, we can fix this."

People ask me all the time what it was that made things click so well between me and Steve Letarte as a driver and crew chief. Steve has an incredible knowledge of how racecars work and how the crew does its job, all of those things. He's done it all and he's worked under some of the greatest crew chiefs of all time and with some of the greatest drivers of all time. But where he clicked with me wasn't building cars or putting in chassis setups. It clicked between us because he knew how to handle me as a person. He didn't talk to me the same way he talked to Jeff Gordon or Jimmie Johnson. He talked to *me*, Dale Junior.

What he realized about me from literally our very first practice session together at Daytona in 2011 was how to keep me focused and motivated. In that practice, I wrecked. But nearly before I was finished spinning, he was already on the radio in my ear, saying, "Dude, don't worry about it. I've got great news. We're already rolling the backup car off the truck; it's even better than the car you're in. We're good, man."

In the four years we worked together he never said to me, "You need to drive better!" Instead, he said, "Okay, here's what I need to do to make this car better, to help you, and for you to help me do that, here's what I need you to do right now." It might have been something in the middle of a race, like, "Dale, I really need you to be running no worse than fifteenth when we hit this last round of pit stops," or in qualifying, like, "Dale, if you run this line around the track on this lap, I think we can pick up X-amount of speed." Steve understood the psychology of giving me a goal to hit and explaining to me why I needed to hit it. He understood the psychology of me.

That's also what makes Micky a great doctor. He gave me the information that I needed to understand what was going on inside my head. He explained to me that it was treatable, that once we had pinpointed the exact signals in my brain that weren't acting normal, he and his team would set up a very specific rehabilitation treatment.

He gave me the rundown of why we were going to do the things that he was about to ask me to do. In other words, he gave me goals. Like Steve, he gave me the plan of attack and brought the people in to start that plan with me. He gave me the what, why, when, and how. When he'd started talking, I was scared to death. By the time he'd finished, I was ready to drop the green flag on this deal.

After our chat, we headed downstairs to the gym. That's right, the gym. Trust me, I was surprised too. And this is where we can erase one of the most common myths about concussion treatment, a myth I still believed until this very moment in Pittsburgh. The days of treating a concussion by telling someone to go lay down in a dark room are over, at least when it comes to the type of symptoms I was having. Put a washcloth on it? That washcloth was thrown in the garbage.

The treatment now is exposure. The idea is not to let the brain rest; it's to make the brain work. Work it out like an injured muscle, with activities that focus on what needs to be fixed. We did heavy physical exercises and we did eye exercises, all designed to make me uncomfortable, to push the limits of what my brain could do. In the end, what we discovered was what I would have to work with as I started my race back to the track. We would find the edge, go over that edge, look at the data, figure out how to push that edge out a little farther, and go at it again.

Kind of sounds like the tire test that landed me there in the first place, doesn't it?

I'll be honest: I wasn't very good at it. At that stage in my life, working out wasn't really my thing. Today, as I write this, I've become a cycling junkie, and I don't ever go anywhere without a bottle of water in my hand. But in October 2012, there were no bikes in my life that didn't have a motor, and the only bottles in my hand were soda and beer. Micky's staff was used to working with Pittsburgh Steelers and Penguins and Pirates, guys who could attack these exercises like machines. But that's not what they were measuring. They were measuring my reaction time, how well my eyes were tracking, how connected my eyes were to the activity of the rest of my body.

I did exercises on the stationary bike, range-of-motion exercises that forced me to track one spot with my eyes while in motion, and a series of balance tests. I also took another ImPACT test. My numbers had already improved pretty dramatically from the test with Dr. Petty the previous week. I met with a vestibular system specialist and, though my left eye showed a little bit of exophoria— that means it went off on its own for a little bit under stress—I was in much better shape, and I had convinced myself that they were going to confirm it. As my anxiety level dropped, just as Micky had explained, so did my symptoms.

When I think back now, the day was hard. Really hard. But a trip that had started out so dang scary ended up being pretty cool. Amy and I got out onto the Steelers practice field and threw the ball around. Then we got our lunch and sat down to eat. The Steelers head coach Mike Tomlin was there too. By day's end Micky's team had evaluated me and given me my homework, a list of exercises I was to do each day. I was to check in with Dr. Petty each day, and Micky gave me his cell phone number and told me to call him to let him know how I was doing or if I ever had any questions. I think back now about how many times I've called him over the years since and wonder if he maybe has regretted that!

Micky told me that if I stuck to my regimen and did what I was assigned, then he was optimistic that I would be back in a racecar soon. I told him that I was being forced to miss two races, that I still wasn't happy about that, and that there wasn't a chance I would miss more than those two. Years later, even after dealing with hundreds of pro athletes, he still talks about how he'd never seen anyone so out of sorts over missing a couple of weeks. Clearly, I was the first racecar driver he'd ever worked with.

Missing those two races was just as miserable as I expected it to be. Actually, it was worse. In 1996, when a broken collarbone forced my dad to pull himself out of his car during the Brickyard 400, he later described watching his famous No. 3 going around the track with someone else behind the wheel as being like "watching your wife going on a date with some other guy." I have to say that Dad's assessment was pretty accurate. Regan Smith finished thirty-sixth at Charlotte after a blown engine, but then he finished seventh at Kansas, no doubt helped by the data we'd collected during my tire test, the one that ended with the crash that had me at home now, doing medicine ball tosses while I watched my car race without me.

The truth was, I felt okay. I really did. Micky's plan was working, and in barely a week's time, I felt fine. I certainly didn't feel as bad as I did after the Kansas or Talladega crashes. What I did feel was kind of stupid. What if I had been honest after Kansas? If I'd missed a race then, maybe we'd still have been in the NASCAR postseason, the Chase, and still have a shot at the championship.

I had to stop myself from going there, from trying to rewind everything. I told myself it was too late for that. Besides, I had to get ready for another test.

Monday, October 22, 2012
Gresham Motorsports Park

The morning after my team finished seventh at Kansas without me, I met them at Gresham Motorsports Park, a cool little short track near Athens, Georgia. We weren't alone. Dr. Jerry Petty was there with us. We ran a ton of laps, with me blasting it as hard as I could, coming into the garage from time to time to talk things through with Steve, but really to be examined by Dr. Petty. He would talk to me, ask me specific questions about my symptoms, and study me to see if there were any signs of any of those symptoms returning, including giving me an on-the-spot eye exam.

He would hold a stick up with a little dot on it and ask me to focus on that dot. Then he'd bring it closer, closer, and closer to my face. If everything is good to go, then your eyes stay locked on that dot and come together as it comes closer, even when the image of it splits into two right in front of your face. If you're still concussed, your eyes just bail, splitting that image way earlier than they should, because the communication pathways have been disrupted. He'd also ask me to close my eyes and tilt my head back. Then he'd give me a push to the shoulder to see how easily I might lose my balance.

I had done all of this in Pittsburgh too. I was locked in. Everything was fine. Even that little bit of exophoria was gone. For me, those tests were a breeze. So was the test on the racetrack.

The next morning Dr. Petty examined me at his office. Everything was still good to go. He called Rick Hendrick, who'd created a little bit of a mess when he told reporters at Kansas that I was already cleared to return the next week. Now, Dr. Petty told him, it was official. We called Micky and gave him the good news. He says now that he was blown away at how quickly I had recovered. He attributed that speed to my dedication to the exercises that I had been given and my willingness to provide the right feedback to both his office and Dr. Petty. He also believed that restoring my confidence had played a huge part in my recovery. I had lowered the anxiety level that he believed had played a big part in making my symptoms worse. Again, his sense of me was spot-on. I wasn't nervous at Gresham. I was too determined to be nervous. (It's interesting now to contrast my feelings about that day at Gresham with the emotions that I felt during a very similar day four years later at Darlington Raceway. File that away—we'll come back to that.) I'd just run 123 laps with the hammer down on a flat, half-mile oval. Our choice of track for that test wasn't a coincidence. It was a lot like the track where my comeback was taking place that weekend.

Sunday, October 28, 2012
Martinsville Speedway

Before the race on Sunday, even before our first practice session on Friday, there Steve and I were again, right back where we had left off with the public two weeks earlier, sitting behind microphones in a racetrack media center. This time it was at Martinsville, the oldest track on the Cup Series calendar and the only track still on the circuit from NASCAR's original schedule in 1948. It was my first time seeing anyone at the racetrack, let alone the media, and I was a little taken aback at the new role I'd been pushed into.

With concussions being such a controversial topic in the sports world, during my two-week absence I don't think I realized how much my name had been attached to that topic. Some people were praising my decision to pull myself out of my car to figure out what was wrong, even though that's not really how it had gone down. I guess others were starting to ask questions about racing like they were asking questions about football. Was I coming back too soon? Was racing too dangerous? That kind of stuff.

Suddenly, whether I wanted to be or not, I was the spokesperson for concussions in auto racing.

I was asked what my two and a half weeks away had been like. "Frustrating . . . as you're waiting on your fogginess to clear up and your symptoms to go away." I was asked if I had considered just parking it for the remainder of the season, for six races instead of only the two. "Just like the decision to get out of the car, I wanted the doctors to make that decision instead of me."

As we went along, I found myself sharing. A lot. I explained about the exercises. I confessed that the two concussions had been totally different injuries. I think that was a shocker to people. I got into the definition of the vestibular system. I talked about the role anxiety plays and described myself as "a mess" because of that anxiety when I'd traveled to Pittsburgh to see Micky. I explained that the Kansas concussion symptoms included fogginess, but the Talladega symptoms involved more irritation. Hey, these same media people were the ones standing right there for my "bloodthirsty" rant, right? I compared racers and football players and layering concussions. I said that the biggest lesson I had learned was that I would be honest with myself and everyone else if I ever found myself in that condition again.

I went on for more than twenty minutes.

If you're fortunate enough to be a professional athlete and then have a long career like I did, you end up doing hundreds of press conferences. Most of them run together. They're run of the mill, with the same questions and the same answers. But then, sometimes, sitting up there you can see the faces of the sportswriters and reporters when something different is happening, when you're really teaching them something. Our weekly NASCAR press conferences are always streamed live over the internet and, on a day like today or at Charlotte when we announced my time off, they are carried on live TV too.

I've always known that my voice has carried some weight, just because of my name and the popularity that's always come with that, and then, thankfully, because we'd had some success on the racetrack. I don't think I realized it right in that moment as it was happening, but that weekend at Martinsville, that was the first time I had a platform to really help people that I hadn't thought about before. All those patients I saw at Micky's—and he sees thousands of patients every year—and how many others who don't go to the doctor? Instead they sit at home, in the fog, just hoping it will clear up one day.

From October 2012 until this day, I've been trying to speak to them.

At one point I was asked if I'd be able to simply climb into my car and get right back up to speed, or would I need a little time to get going. I said I felt like I'd been gone a year, so I'd be jumping in the gas right from the first lap. The truth was a little less bold. On Sunday, we ran okay and I kept it in the middle third of the field. Steve rolled out some killer pit strategy and had us in a position for me to make a late run into the top ten, but it didn't happen. I finished twenty-first, but on the lead lap. He was pretty steamed, but after the race, when he started grilling me in the garage about why I didn't take advantage of what he'd done, I reminded him that I'd been gone for two weekends and, like it or not, that day had been a test session for me. I might have talked a big game on Friday, but on Sunday I did indeed need a little bit of time to prove to myself that I was okay to be back out there. The next weekend I finished seventh on the fastest, hairiest intermediate track we run, Texas Motor Speedway, and I closed out 2012 with another top-ten finish, at Homestead-Miami Speedway.

In 2013, we didn't win a race, but in my fourteenth full season

I had perhaps my most consistent year. I set a personal best with twenty-two top-ten finishes in thirty-six races, including a second place run in the Daytona 500, and I finished fifth in the championship standings, my best finish in nearly a decade. Me, Steve, the whole No. 88 team—we were clicking, man. Steve told me that he believed, as awful as it had been, that us enduring the concussion issues of 2012 had been the best thing that could have happened to us when it came to creating a bond. We weren't just coworkers; we were really good friends. We'd experienced something together, and we were stronger for it. It was also showing at the racetrack. We both knew 2014 was going to be huge.

At the season-ending NASCAR awards dinner in Las Vegas, I was asked, for the first time in a long time, about my 2012 concussions. The reporter wanted to know if I had experienced any symptoms lately. I answered no.

"In fact," I told him, "now that I think back on it, I don't think we wrecked at all, hard or soft, all year, did we? I feel great. I haven't felt foggy since Talladega 2012. It doesn't really even cross my mind."

I was at peace.

That was about to change.

CHAPTER 4

THE CLOUD RETURNS

Sunday, February 23, 2014
Daytona International Speedway

I don't care how long you race for a living—you can do it for decades, for a thousand races—there will still be only one or two times in your career where you take the checkered flag and go, *Man, that day was dang near perfect.*

The 2014 Daytona 500 was one of those days. It didn't necessarily start off that way. We started the race ninth, and it rained a bunch. After the start we ended up delayed for six hours, and when the race finally got going, the No. 88 car didn't lead until the race was nearly three-quarters done. But once we got to the front, we were awesome. Nobody had anything for us. If anyone ever took the lead from me, I'd take it right back. I led six different times and had to hold off the whole field after a late restart. Brad Keselowski came after me on the last lap, but my teammate Jeff Gordon helped push me to the win. The Daytona 500, man!

That win made a lot of statements. It was my twentieth career Cup Series victory. Guys who have done that, that's a small club. It was my second Daytona 500 win. That's an even smaller club. It also snapped a fifty-five-race winless streak. Most importantly, this was the first year that NASCAR had its win-and-in postseason format. That meant that even though we were only one race into the season, we were all but guaranteed to be one of the sixteen teams competing for the championship that fall.

That was the biggest statement of them all. We had announced to the garage that after the consistency and the momentum we'd built over the previous three years, 2014 was what we had been building toward, and they had better be ready. My exact quote standing in Victory Lane that night was, "We are going for the jugular this year."

These feelings were a big improvement from how I'd felt just one month earlier. That's when the news broke that Steve Letarte would be leaving our team at the end of 2014 to become a TV analyst for NBC Sports. I'd actually known about it before the public found out. My fan base—Junior Nation—was devastated. But not as devastated as me.

The day I found out, I cried. I went to him and I let him have it. "Man, why are you doing this to us?!" I couldn't believe that he was going to bail, not now, not as I was experiencing this career resurgence, feeling so great on the track and finally feeling just as great off the track. But he had two kids at home that he never saw. He was killing himself to try to keep up with the crew chiefs of the other title contenders, especially Chad Knaus, his mentor, who called the shots for Jimmie Johnson's seven-time championship team right there out of the same race shop we worked out of. I got it. I knew why he was doing it. But I didn't have to like it.

Steve and I agreed that instead of worrying about what life was going to be like apart, we would focus on making sure we got everything out of the time we had left. We still had a whole season to work together. We could worry about 2015 when the time came, so we agreed that we were going to run 2014 like we had nothing to lose, because that's exactly what we had. That's how we ran the Daytona 500, and after we won it, we *really* had nothing to lose. We were in the postseason, so we threw caution to the wind. When we had a chance to win, we could roll the dice to make that happen. If we didn't have a shot to win, we could try stuff in races to see if it would or wouldn't work when we went back to those same tracks in the fall.

It was awesome.

We started the year with three straight top-two finishes. We won four races, the most I'd won in a single season since 2004. We spent the entire twenty-six-race regular season ranked in the top five and ended the year with an eighth-place finish in the championship, the third time in four years we'd finished in the top eight in the points standings and our fourth straight season in the postseason.

But behind those numbers was an ugly truth. I was having symptoms again. Remember those notes I told you about at the start of this book? This was the season when I started taking those notes.

I know what you're thinking. I had promised I wouldn't keep those kinds of secrets again. I had promised it in 2002 and I had promised it in 2012, to myself, my team, my family, and the public. During my comeback press conference at Martinsville, after missing the two races, I said to the world: "This has definitely changed the way I feel about it. If I know I've suffered another concussion or

I know I have symptoms after an accident, I'm definitely going to be a lot more responsible about it."

That promise was easy to stick to in 2013, when there were no symptoms. In 2014, in a position to maybe finally win a championship, I broke that promise. I was keeping secrets about what was happening inside my head. Again.

Monday, April 7, 2014
Texas Motor Speedway

The first notes came seven weeks after the Daytona 500 win, when I ran into the wet grass and had my frontstretch crash at Texas Motor Speedway, dot-dot-dotting along the wall. As I wrote in the notes app of my iPhone, I felt foggy almost instantly. The other word I used was *trapped*. That's a man that is thinking, *After nearly two years of feeling fine, now this?!*

With that slight return of my concussion symptoms came a much more significant return—my anxiety. When I think back on it now, I realize that worry over the fact that one day my symptoms might return, I guess it never really went away. It was always in the back of my mind, whether I realized it or not. I took down only one note between my return at the end of 2012 and the Texas race in April 2014; it was after the Daytona 300 Xfinity Series race on February 23, 2013. People remember that race for the scary crash at the finish line when Kyle Larson got airborne and his car ripped the catchfence apart at the start-finish line. I was caught up in that wreck too. All I wrote was, "Slammed wall at finish line during Larson flip. Had headache and pressure all night. Felt fine Sunday for the 500."

Over that time I continued following the NFL controversy with CTE but also continued to stay in touch with Micky. I referred several other racecar drivers to him so they could be checked out. I answered a lot of questions from both the media and even some of my fellow competitors about concussions and how they are diagnosed and treated, especially when NASCAR made changes to its concussion-related policies. At the start of the 2014 season it became mandatory that all drivers do baseline concussion screenings. Some of the guys complained about that publicly, so naturally the media came to me for a reaction. Now I was NASCAR's unofficial concussion spokesperson. I had "earned" that job because I had been through it and had healed. Now, though, I wasn't so sure about the healed part.

My anxiety over that is apparent in my notes from the days after the Texas crash:

Went home feeling a slight headache and visual issues like erratic eye movement. Not being able to focus on a single point or object. More than slight air-headedness or grogginess.

Spent night on couch with Amy. Got tired and went to bed. Felt trapped in my head some, but just slightly. Couldn't focus or remember simple things. Worried about my head all the time and couldn't plug in to my surroundings.

Groggy head Tuesday AM, over 12 hrs after accident. Emotional frustrations then too.

"Emotional frustrations"—there's that anxiety.

Wednesday noon, still some slight mental mistakes or slip-ups. Walked into a clear glass wall I thought was a door while focusing hard on racing mural, looking for my car in it. Could be a "throw it in the concussion bin" moment but I think it's still just a slight lack of mental sharpness that will be better by Friday.

We had a test session at Michigan Speedway, and as I was walking into the door of the media center, I eyed a mural featuring a bunch of racecars and victory celebrations. I'd won there twice, including a huge win just two years earlier, and I was looking to see if my victories were included in the artwork. The walls of that building are all glass, and I walked right into one of them "Tommy Boy"–style.

That misjudgment might have been concussion-related, an inability to focus. Or it might have just been a dumb mistake that I would've made anyway. I certainly wasn't the first person to walk into a super-clean glass wall. But that's what having concussion anxiety can do to you. It makes you question why you do or don't do certain things. Micky calls it "throwing it into the concussion bin"—you just naturally kind of blame it on the condition, fair or not.

So is that pressure I'm feeling inside my skull for real, or am I just imagining it because I'm super sensitive and stressed? Or is it real, not all that bad, and am I making it worse because I'm super sensitive and stressed? This is the cycle I would find myself stuck in whenever I thought I was feeling symptoms. It's exhausting, and it never really goes away after you suffer through something like I did in 2012. Every day is a constant checklist. Every morning you make sure everything works okay, and the rest of the day you wonder if simple mistakes are indicators of bigger problems. *Man, I don't remember where I left my car keys* or *I have a small headache* becomes *Is my memory failing?!* or *Is my brain injured again?!*

You can also read in my post-Texas notes ". . . but I think it's still just slight lack of mental sharpness that will be better by Friday." There's another cycle, the one I was used to from 1998 and 2002, and any other time I believe I was concussed. Most of the time, it improved by race weekend. But the race weekend itself had something to do with that. Micky and Dr. Petty both say that the focus it takes to do the job of a racecar driver sharpens your mind. It finds a way to shut off those nagging, mild symptoms because it has to in order to achieve the super-intense level of concentration a racer must have. Any of my former crew chiefs will tell you the same was true of me even when there weren't any concussions! Steve Letarte likes to remind me that nearly all of my pit road penalties—dumb stuff like breaking the pit road speed limit or overshooting my pit stall and sliding through the box where my crew was waiting to do their thing—those mistakes almost never happened in the real heat of an in-race battle. No, they happened when the race was under a caution flag or I was pitting by myself, the non-pressure situations. Why? Because I wasn't as focused up.

That helps to explain the strangest pattern from my notes. Like from that Michigan test:

Test session . . . both Tuesday and Wednesday, when I was in the car I felt sharper than when I wasn't. But when I drove on the highway Tuesday with sunglasses I felt odd and not sharp. Removing sunglasses makes it much better.

So on the road driving a rental car—eye issues, that swishy feeling of my brain lagging behind my vision. Then, on the racetrack traveling 200 mph—no eye issues, always hitting my marks, and constantly collecting data on how the car is running.

That's a pattern that continued on a much larger scale throughout 2014: sharp on the track, but shaky off. After the Texas scare I finished second at Darlington and seventh at Richmond. The next was the Talladega event when I chose to bail in the closing laps. After a week of stress and no sleep worrying about how I handled

Talladega, we cranked out ten top-ten finishes over the next dozen races, including a pair of wins at Pocono Raceway. But by summer's end, the fog was back.

Saturday, August 23, 2014
Bristol Motor Speedway

In the legendary night race at Bristol, a half-mile oval shaped like a giant cereal bowl, I was forced to open up my iPhone and jot down more notes. Roughly one-third of the way into the 500-lap race, leader Denny Hamlin got knocked out of the lead by Kevin Harvick, slid all the way down the frontstretch, and came back onto the track at the entrance of the first turn. I drove all the way up to the top of the track to try to get by him, but he smacked the driver's side of my Chevy. Like a can opener, he peeled the sheet metal off that whole side of the car. The hit felt like nothing. It looked like nothing. But, looking at my notes, it didn't feel like nothing. You can tell I was surprised and confused by what it triggered.

> Hit Denny in turn one.
>
> Immediately after the wreck I felt the very slightest mental oddness. Not trapped, not foggy. Just feeling anxiety of being judged. Felt people were really studying me and I had extra anxiety for that and worried if I'd done any physical damage. Got back in the car and drove. Drove good but it took me a second to zap back into my surroundings. Felt like a dream for a second. I wasn't super sharp and "on time" but could handle repetition easy. From the time of the wreck until I went to bed I had a moderate to slight headache. Didn't take any meds.

I went to bed that night but couldn't go to sleep. That's not unusual for me, especially after a Bristol race. I told you my mind never stops. It's always the loudest when I'm in bed. This night, it was particularly loud.

> I had no rapid eye movement. I didn't feel trapped. Maybe a very faint feeling of trapped or really not being able to escape my own thoughts. The "voice" in my head or thoughts I have are much louder than normal.
>
> I took a sleeping pill and went to bed. Woke up to pee around 2 AM and had some problems going back to sleep due to the loud thoughts. I have loud thoughts normally, so this isn't crazy.
>
> Woke up Sunday. Feeling 95%. The 5% is slight head ache and just knowing I had a hit and overanalyzing myself. Compared to Texas I think I'm gonna be ok?
>
> 100% by 5 pm Sunday. Monday–Thursday no issues.

Even after finishing thirty-ninth at Bristol, we were third in the championship standings. I ran good but not great heading into the ten-race postseason, and three races into that postseason we were among the championship leaders.

Sunday, October 5, 2014
Kansas Speedway

Nearing the halfway mark of the race, we were leading. Okay, we weren't just leading—we were cruising. I was about to lead my forty-sixth lap and had a full two-second lead over second place Joey Logano. Rolling toward the exit of the fourth turn, there was a pop. The right front tire had blown. I smacked the wall flush with the whole right side of the car, just flattening it. The guys fixed the car as best they could, and we got back out to finish the day 63 laps down in thirty-ninth place. This is what I wrote after the race. You'll see I'd found a new way to describe my fogginess as I finished the race, traveled home, and attended a charity golf tournament the next day.

No headache after the crash. Felt little drunk, 1/2 of a beer. But got in car and returned to the track and felt fine out there.

After the race I got out of the car and felt 1 or 2 beers drunk, but still no pain. No rapid eye movement or any other symptoms.

I have some slight coordination problems such as typing or fastening a belt because of the drunkenness.

No eye focus or rapid eye movement issues. I double state that because I feel like that is the first symptom in a definite problem.

By the end of the plane ride I felt much less drunk. The drunk is still the only symptom. Neck seems like it might get sore. Really flinched hard to keep my head from flying into the headrest.

Driving home there was an increase in drunk feeling. Basically, when I take my eyes off the road I would get woozy. But overall even though I felt drunk today, I felt happy drunk. Driving home some headlights did bother my eyes. As soon as I got home and into the house the drunk feeling decreased quickly back to 1/2 beer.

Played Madden. Felt forgetful in one game but sharp in a second game.

Monday morning. Took a while to wake up. Focus on single objects was tough on drive to airport. Felt slight groggy feeling. Not really fog. Just sluggish. Took about an hour to get out of that. By noon I was feeling 90%. No headache. No eye issues. Just feel a little flighty or airheaded. 1/4 beer drunk.

Felt decent at the golf tournament. Like I was 1 beer in. I did have a beer and felt the effects from it were a bit exaggerated. Hadn't ate lunch. It was 2 pm.

Was 100% next day.

The next two weekends we ran well at Charlotte and Talladega, leading laps at both, but left with a pair of bad finishes. My drunken feelings had gone away and weren't an issue. They certainly weren't a factor by the end of the month.

Sunday, October 26, 2014
Martinsville Speedway

In the season's third-from-last race, I had a day that was as much fun as you can possibly have driving a racecar. There was a late restart and Tony Stewart had the lead. That guy always reminded people of my father, and with good reason. He's one of the toughest racers I've ever seen, especially at places like the flat, gritty half-mile at Martinsville.

But that racetrack is so special for so many reasons, because of the history of the track and my father's history running there. Winning there earns you what might be the best trophy in professional sports, a grandfather clock. My dad won six of them. I remember one of them sitting in the hallway as you came into the house, just by the stairs, with an oval-shaped rug in front of it. That's where I would spend Sunday afternoons, racing my Matchbox cars around that rug and listening to the radio blasting through the house with a broadcast of my father off racing somewhere. Richard Petty and Darrell Waltrip won at Martinsville so many times that Waltrip used to joke that around his house at noon and midnight, everyone for miles would be woken up from all his grandfather clocks chiming at once. I grew up going to races at Martinsville and watching all those guys jamming into the brakes and jamming into each other, me playing in the infield with my friends while Dad raced.

I wasn't greedy. I didn't need six grandfather clocks. I just wanted one of them. With only three laps remaining, I smoked by Smoke (that's what we call Tony Stewart) and grabbed that win.

It wasn't enough to get us back into the championship hunt. We ended finishing eighth in the final standings. But that win at Martinsville was my fourth of the year. It fulfilled a lifelong dream and put a grandfather clock in my den. I was also happy to finally add to the amazing Martinsville win total of my boss, Rick Hendrick. It was his twenty-second win at the NASCAR track that's also in his home state of Virginia. His first win as a team owner came there in 1984, a win that saved his tiny new operation from going under. From Geoff Bodine and Darrell Waltrip to Jeff Gordon and Jimmie Johnson, Hendrick Motorsports had experienced some of the greatest days of its existence at Martinsville.

It also experienced its worst day. On October 23, 2004, a Hendrick Motorsports plane went down in the hills near the race-track, carrying friends and family to that day's race. All ten aboard were killed, including Rick's brother, John, his two nieces, and also his only son and my good friend, Ricky Hendrick. When my dad was killed at Daytona in 2001, Rick Hendrick was there for me.

When he lost Ricky three years later, I tried to be there for him. That's a bond that will never go away and was only strengthened when Rick hired me to drive for him three years after the plane crash. When I was a kid, he pushed a napkin across the table and asked me to sign it, claiming that it was a binding contract and one day, after I grew up, I would drive for him. When I made the decision to leave my only NASCAR employer—my father's company, Dale Earnhardt Incorporated—Hendrick Motorsports was the only place I ever intended to go.

Now, on the tenth anniversary of that worst day of his life, it meant so much to me to be able to bring a smile to Rick Hendrick's face.

That win was also the perfect sendoff for Steve Letarte. He was a Hendrick Motorsports lifer, having made his way up from sweeping the floors to calling the shots for Jeff Gordon and then me. So Martinsville meant a lot to him too. But if there was any sadness to that day, or to the two races that followed it, this is where it came from—knowing that Steve and I were done. It had been two years ago that very weekend when we had to sit together in the Martinsville Speedway media center and answer questions about my comeback from the two races off. Now I felt fine. I hadn't added any new notes to the iPhone in the three weeks since Kansas, and I wouldn't add anything new to those notes for nearly another year.

Greg Ives took over as crew chief in 2015. His approach was much different than Steve's had been. Greg is an engineer, so he approaches everything—including me—like that. We're all part of the equation he's working on. Steve was a motivator. Greg is a mathematician. I don't think one is right or wrong; they just aren't the same approach. Because of that, the 2015 season felt a lot different, but results-wise, we picked right up where we'd left off. We nearly won the Daytona 500 again and started the year with a bunch of top-six finishes.

I had a couple of crashes early and didn't take down a single note from either one of them, but my anxiety was high all year. For whatever reason, that season seemed to have more crashes than most and it always felt like they were right on top of me. I was uneasy all the time. It never felt like I could go more than two months or so without someone hitting me. Still, I had no serious concussion symptoms during the first half of the season, at least none that I thought were worthy of taking notes about.

What is interesting is that when you go back and see what I was saying in my weekly press conferences, before and after races, I sound downright nostalgic. I think that's a pretty big indicator that I was beginning to think about the end of my career, and it was probably happening much sooner than later.

Sunday, May 3, 2015
Talladega Superspeedway

I was feeling particularly nostalgic when we got to Talladega, the tenth race of the season. On Friday I started telling the media stories about being a kid and hanging out in the Talladega infield with my buddy Brad Means, son of Jimmy "Smut" Means, scavenging for parts and pieces and racing stuff. That race always seems to fall on the same week as my father's birthday, April 29, and in 2015 he would have turned sixty-four. I would love to tell you that I had commemorated that during past race weeks, but I hadn't. That changed when I got to the track where he'd won ten times, the all-time record. It really changed by the end of Sunday's race. We won.

Like Daytona, this win did a lot. It finally got me back in Victory Lane at that track for the first time in eleven years. That got the fans off Greg's back, at least for a little bit. But it also finally allowed me to let go of what I'd done there one year earlier, the day I'd lifted and felt so guilty about it. Anyone who was there this time around and saw me lead the race five different times—not to mention the way I dictated the pace and altered everyone else's decision-making—there was no way anyone who saw that was still going to point to what I did in 2014 and say I'd lost my guts.

After the race, I started reminiscing again. "When we won today, it made me think about my dad's birthday, how much I miss him, and how much he meant to me and so many more people. I can't even think about the number of folks that he had a relationship with, and all his fans out there who really enjoyed seeing him compete here."

Just two months later, we won the Firecracker 400 at Daytona from the pole position. We totally dominated. I'd swept the 2015 Daytona races, and this win came just two weeks after I'd asked Amy to marry me. I did it in Germany while we were there with Kelley and her husband, L.W., doing some genealogical research on the Earnhardt family. I proposed in a Lutheran church that my family attended three hundred years ago.

It was a great summer. We started the postseason ranked fifth in the standings. My first three seasons after I joined Hendrick Motorsports, I felt like we were always playing catch-up. Now, for the fourth straight year we hit September feeling like legit title contenders. Unfortunately, after the very first practice session of the very first race of that postseason, I had my notes app back open. And it would stay open all fall.

Saturday, September 19, 2015
Chicagoland Speedway

On paper, Chicagoland looks like Kansas or Charlotte or Texas, any of the other one-and-a-half-mile intermediate tracks we run. But the term fans like to use—*cookie cutter*—that's not really accurate. Every track has its own personality and quirks, good and bad.

Chicagoland is bumpy. There's one big bump right in the bottom racing groove, and it is torture. In an effort to keep our cars glued to the ground, we run them really low in the front. Beneath the nose of each racecar there's also an aerodynamic wing—a scoop, really—that looks like a shelf. That's the splitter. If you're a long-time fan of mine, then you know that Mr. Splitter and me, we aren't friends. That was especially true at Chicago, where that low car with that splitter would hit that bump, and it was just like *BANG*. It was really jarring.

> First practice. Had a very harsh ride. Bump into Turn One was a drop for the whole car. Bumps into Turns 3/4 are mainly splitter in the middle and right side headlight. Made me feel drugged, foggy, drunk, sleepy. Couldn't "wake up" and "clear up." Gave me a slight tight headache. Time 1:30.

Every time I hit that bump my head would bang against the headrest of my seat. It felt like a big drop before whamming into the ground and into my head, a drop that sat right in the racing lane that was the fastest line around the racetrack, waiting for me every single time I came through that turn. *Wham. Wham. Wham.* On Sunday in the race that could happen as many as four hundred times.

My brain at this point of the season and my life was still fragile. Subjecting it to a repeated, carbon-copied pounding all day, all I could think was that it was going to be no different than an NFL lineman hitting his head the same way on every snap in the trenches.

> Got out of car took a Goody's shot and felt this way for around one hour. Started clearing up after that hour. 90 minutes after still not totally clear. Standing up and walking helps.
>   Ran second practice. At 5 pm I felt 95%.

I told Greg that either he had to figure out a way to improve the ride quality of the racecar or he'd have to watch me steer around that bump all day on Sunday. He and the team worked with me, and we finished a respectable twelfth.

Sunday, October 11, 2015
Charlotte Motor Speedway

We came to our hometown track at Charlotte as one of the twelve drivers all tied for the points lead, thanks to NASCAR's new playoff-style bracket postseason format. But by day's end we were already essentially eliminated from contention because we had a brutally awful race. I hit the wall three different times. The hardest came when there was oil on the track that hadn't been cleaned up, and I pancaked the right side of the car. Again, it looked like nothing. My notes tell you otherwise.

> Hit oil and slammed wall. Instant headache. Felt lazy and 1 beer drunk rest of the day.

Monday-Thursday felt ok but have slight pressure head-ache. No eye issues. Could fumble some speech and mind was very forgetful. Don't consider this one as serious as some I had in 2014.

For the first time, I felt as bad late in the week as I did in the days immediately following the race.

Thursday I felt hungover and frustrated all day. Drank some water and really improved.

Friday I seemed to wake up really slow and feel groggy and not sharp. Gets better after a few hours. Weird how I feel worse Thursday and Friday as compared to earlier in the week. I did drink Sunday and Tuesday pretty heavily. May be dehydration. Water does seem to clear up the cobwebs a bit but I still feel nervous about my situation and not sure if I'm really sharp. The three different hits into the wall that Sunday were 20, 13, and 23 Gs.

I had gone to the team and NASCAR and we'd gotten the black box numbers from my three hits at Charlotte, what all looked like glancing blows. None had crossed over into what is considered the threshold of a big hit, that 25-plus G load. None of them had come anywhere close to my big 40-G hit at Kansas in 2012; only one was even slightly more than halfway there. But the fact that my symptoms were still lingering as we arrived at the next track on the schedule—that scared me. It scared me bad. That nervousness I'd felt early in the season—that I couldn't get clear of any wreck with-out finding myself in the middle of yet another—that was worse now. I was wrecking more often, and even when I wasn't, I was constantly worried about when the next hit was coming and how it might make me feel. I never felt healed. I felt vulnerable.

Sunday, October 18, 2015
Kansas Speedway

That stress is reflected in the big-picture tone of my next set of notes. My anxiety was back in a big way. It wasn't helped by being at this particular track where we were racing next.

> Felt good Friday after qualifying.
>
> Saturday was feeling great all day.
>
> Wake up in the mornings with slight headache that's similar to a sinus pressure, this goes away after an hour of being up and active. Every morning has been a real challenge with worry about my future, how I'm changed now, how much of myself will I never recover.
>
> Sunday morning thought a week after Charlotte: There's a lot of things I do today that frustrate me. Mid-sentence, not being able to find the words to finish. Remembering simple things, short-term memory being the most common. Some of it I'm sure is just stress, getting old, and so on. But when in vocal conversation I choose the wrong word or can't find the word to complete my thought, that makes me so sad and scared.

We finished twenty-first at Kansas, one lap down. I was happy just to get out of there. Now we were headed to the place where I had won just six months earlier but had also experienced so much anxiety the year before that.

Sunday, October 25, 2015
Talladega Superspeedway

I had no idea at the time, but these feelings of pressure—not the emotional pressure, the physical sinus pressure—that I was beginning to record in my notes, they were a sneak preview of what was to come in the not-too-distant future.

> Two weeks after Charlotte, Friday at Dega. Really felt laggy and slow. Slightly wobbly even. I don't know why this is, haven't felt this all week. Have a ton of anxiety about several media things I'm doing this entire weekend. But parts of the day I'm ok, but other times I feel kinda drunk. I'm real nervous my speech and mannerisms are going to reflect this so I'm really anxious in company. I have had moments of soreness in my sinus areas, around my eyes, behind my nose on one side or the other. High cheeks area near my temple beside my eyes. Not really my forehead though.

Even still, I finished second in the race at Talladega.

We went to Martinsville the following weekend, and again my late-week anxiety took over. I barely slept the Thursday night before going to the racetrack. During Friday's practice I hit a big bump that rattled my head similar to what happened at Chicagoland, but not nearly as much of an event. My nighttime headaches continued all weekend as did that nagging sinus pressure, though now it had extended into my jaw hinge and temples. Another practice jolt caused my head to smack back and forth between the headrests of my seat. It took a half-hour after practice to shake those cobwebs. But again, I finished near the front, this time a solid fourth-place run.

In fact, we finished the season with four top-six finishes over the last five races and even won the season's next-to-last race, at Phoenix International Raceway. Our twelfth-place finish in the final championship standings was disappointing, but we'd posted three wins, and in my sixteenth full-time season, I had matched my career bests with sixteen top-five finishes and twenty-two top tens. On top of that, Amy and I were planning a wedding, now one year away.

I had every reason to spend that winter feeling great about where I was, personally and professionally. However, I was eaten up inside. I'd spent the 2014 and '15 seasons keeping secrets about my health. Again. And I felt very guilty about that. I was a hypocrite and I knew it. I think, deep down, that's why I was keeping those notes on my phone. As I told you earlier, I realize now that I was basically leaving a trail of bread crumbs for someone to find in case something really bad happened to me, so people could see what I had been fighting, even if it was after the fact. It was also just a personal sounding board. I had to get it off my chest somewhere and tell someone, even if that someone was an iPhone app.

I'm willing to admit now that I was hiding my symptoms at the same time I was telling people that other drivers shouldn't hide theirs. I had fallen right back into that old-school racing mentality. Tape an aspirin to it, tape your eyelids open, put a washcloth on it, write it into your iPhone when no one was looking—whatever it took to stay in the racecar, especially when it was running so well.

But time was running out on my charade. The 2016 season had arrived. My secrets were about to be exposed to the world.

CHAPTER 5

THE LOST SEASON

2016

I get asked all the time now, when was it that I really, seriously started to think about retirement? It was probably earlier and more often than you think.

In 2009 and '10 I had some pretty low moments. Those were my second and third seasons with Hendrick Motorsports. I'd left the company my father founded after twelve years—though it wasn't really that company anymore—to drive for the most powerful organization in NASCAR, and I ran pretty terrible. It wasn't that we didn't win races; we weren't even finishing in the top twenty in the championship standings. I felt like I was letting so many people down, from Rick to my sponsors that were spending millions to support me to my fan base. Privately, I was telling my closest friends and family that I still loved racing, but I wasn't having any fun. Racing is supposed to be fun, right? So why would I keep being miserable? At the lowest points during that stretch, sometimes I would daydream of just cashing out and going to live in the Caribbean or something. I had plenty of money. I could just go be a beach bum.

But the same reasons that I felt so miserable were also why I wouldn't let myself quit. I didn't want to let down the people who believed in me, and I certainly didn't want to turn my back on the people who depended on me to make their living. Between Hendrick Motorsports and JR Motorsports and all the companies who either sponsored us or helped us out in whatever we did, I couldn't just cut and run on them. Same goes for Junior Nation, the people who wear my name and face on their clothes or have big 88s and 8s tattooed on their bodies. The people on my team and supporting my team— they are the reasons I stuck it out during the lean times.

I also wanted to make sure my legacy wasn't just this huge letdown. "Well, Dale Junior, he was pretty good at the start of his career, but then he just sucked and then he disappeared." We fixed that. From 2011 through '15, our performance was finally where it should have been. We made the postseason field every year. We led the points standings six different times. We had twenty-plus top-ten finishes four times. We won seven races in '14–'15, despite switching crew chiefs in the middle of it. And we accomplished all of that even while I silently suffered through big chunks of '12, '14, and '15.

Still, throughout 2015, during conversations at my office with Kelley and Mike Davis, I tried to drop hints that we needed to start thinking about an exit strategy. Kelley, as you know, runs every aspect of my businesses. Mike has worked with me for more than a decade, first as a public relations rep and now overseeing our brand management at JRM and running all our media efforts. He's the guy you hear as my cohost on our *Dale Jr. Download* podcast every week. He's a great friend and a real confidant.

I'd just blurt out to them, "Hey, y'all, I want to quit." But I don't think it ever really computed with them how serious I was. I suppose the timing made no sense to them. I was finally running well in my Cup car on Sundays, and our JR Motorsports teams were doing well on Saturdays in the NASCAR Xfinity Series. More importantly, they thought I was totally healthy, more than three years removed from my 2012 injuries. They had no idea what I was going through every time I got hit on the track. Because of that, even when I would try to be as blunt as I could and say, "Listen, I need to quit before something really bad happens to me!" they would just look at me like, "Well, what bad is going to happen? Why are you thinking this way?"

I couldn't make them understand my sense of urgency because I was never being fully honest with them. I never told them how bad I really felt. I never showed them the notes I had been taking. In fact, I think the first time my sister will have seen my notes about my symptoms is right now, at the same time as y'all, when she reads this book. I think they probably assumed I was tired or hungover or I was just being a whiny racecar driver.

At home, Amy knew I was thinking about quitting driving because we talked about it a lot. She was eager for me to put a date on it and kind of officially start the countdown, but not because she wanted me to stop racing. She was worried about me. I hadn't shared my notes with her, either. Not yet anyway. But even as hard as I tried to hide it, she could tell when I wasn't feeling right after a race. Not all the time, but enough to be worried about her soon-to-be husband.

Even with all of that weighing on my mind, we hit the 2016 season with a lot of optimism. My teammate Jimmie Johnson was once again considered the favorite to win the Cup title, looking to tie my father's record of seven. Jeff Gordon had retired at the end of 2015, nearly winning the championship in his final race. I was envious of how he'd gone out and thought maybe I could do the same. His replacement was Chase Elliott, son of NASCAR Hall of Famer Bill Elliott, one of my dad's biggest rivals. Chase had driven for us and won an Xfinity Series championship. Kasey Kahne was back too. My crew was fully intact, led by Greg Ives, and there was no reason to believe that we wouldn't continue our momentum from the previous five seasons.

Early in the season-opening Daytona 500 my car broke loose as I was trying to work the draft through Turn 4, and I ended up sliding into the massive wall that leads to the entrance to pit road. I went straight in, nose-first, and bent that whole nose in flat, like a boxer had punched my Chevy with a straight jab. I made no notes that day or that week. *Okay*, I thought, *that's good*. Health-wise, I was already ahead of where I'd left off in 2015.

Over the next eight races we never finished lower than fourteenth, with three runner-up finishes, and were ranked solidly in the top ten as we hit the middle of spring.

Sunday, May 1, 2016
Talladega Superspeedway

This was a bad day nearly from the start. Only fifty laps into the race, I had an aerodynamic deal like at Daytona. I tried to make a move but ended up looping it, this time on the backstretch. While I was sideways I caught hits from a couple of cars, including my teammate Kahne, but there weren't any bad hits until near the end of the race. I had my repaired Chevy back on the racetrack and riding in the high lane as we entered the first turn. But Carl Edwards, also back out there with a repaired ride, broke a suspension part, and his car suddenly snapped a hard right toward the wall—right in front of me. I hit him so hard it nearly ripped the front quarter of my car clean off. Instantly, the old symptoms were back, as I recorded in my notes:

> Carl's suspension broke and we hit the wall hard. Car rolls to the grass and I exit quickly. I immediately felt like my bell was rung. Don't remember what I did with my gloves. Lost them. Small headache. Drunk, one beer feeling. Eye movement seemed sharp and ok.
>
> On flight home I am staring off, deep in thought. Worrying a lot. Went home and rested. Did not sleep well the night before the race so a nap made me feel much better.

On Monday morning, I noticed a new symptom. I had significant pain in my sinuses. This was way more than the sinus pressure I had felt before. It was a feeling that would end up dogging me all spring and summer.

> Monday-Tuesday I felt 95% better. Still some aches. Sinus areas aching. Eyeball sore. Behind the eyes sore. Temples sore. Some pains coming and going around the skull. Some moments (an hour here and there) of getting very tired and mentally exhausted followed by moments of feeling good and clear.

I jumped in my street car and drove to a studio to record some radio ads for Goodyear.

> Driving a car, I felt lazy mentally. I didn't have any real moment of feeling "off" till I had to read some liners for Goodyear. I

struggled with picking up the next word of each sentence as well as I usually do. This scared me. That was the only red flag most of the week.

I can read articles well. I can plug into a conversation fine. I feel really close to 100%, like 95%, but that 5% is still not there come Wednesday morning. Wednesday morning wake up 7:30 with slight headache or pressure and a light beer buzz. My disposition mainly has been happy. No mood issues.

Here I am going through my personal systems check again. Was I triggered emotionally as I had been at Talladega in 2012? No. But was the anxiety returning, my worry about the bigger picture of what I was experiencing? Yes.

I felt like this hit was a hard one and that after the wreck I was concerned that this concussion was worse than most I've felt in the last 2 years. But honestly, it's been no more severe. Oddly, similar to Charlotte 2015, I feel like Wednesday I didn't make any gains from Tuesday or Monday. Could Thursday and Friday be worse with anxiety and stress increased?

Thursday. Feeling fine mentally. Still carrying some headache and pain. It's more in my forehead and temples and sides than the sinus pains of a day or two ago.

Friday wake up with small headache. But feel really good overall.

We got through the next race at Kansas Speedway without incident, finishing fifteenth. At our next stop I wasn't so lucky.

Sunday, May 15, 2016
Dover International Speedway

Dover is the track you'd get if you took the concrete cereal bowl short track of Bristol and put it on a stretching rack. It's just as crazy and just as hard to stay out of trouble, only it's a full mile long instead of Bristol's half-mile. With forty-six laps remaining, Jimmie Johnson was the leader, but he couldn't get up to speed on a restart. He stalled and puttered along as everyone was jumping into the gas, so the field had to just as quickly jump into the brakes. It was a total mess. Cars started spinning and wrecking everywhere, right at the entrance to the first turn.

I had restarted back in the pack. When all the wrecking started sliding down the banking, I hit the top lane and, amazingly, was in the clear. I'd made it all the way into Turn 1, but Casey Mears came out of nowhere, up all the way from the bottom of the track, blasting up the banking and hitting my left front corner so hard it lifted us both off the ground. The blow pushed my car into the wall for another hard lick, this time to the right front corner. Bang and *BANG*. My head smacked back and forth between the headrests of my seat. As I slid into the little patch of grass at the bottom of the turn, I was panicked, but as my notes tell you, I was relatively okay after my third hard hit in three weeks.

Got my head banged around in a crash on the frontstretch. It was on a restart and we were nowhere near full speed. Still was enough to shake me up a little. Not real bad though. No headache or pressure. Very very light symptoms if any. No issues during the week. Zero.

The next week was a fourteenth-place finish in the 600-miler at Charlotte, followed by a second place run at Pocono. We led late in the day, but I just didn't have anything for Kurt Busch. After the race I told the media that I was bummed about having no wins on the year, but that we'd finished second four times now in fourteen races and that victory felt inevitable. A reporter pointed out that I now had twenty-six career Cup Series wins, but thirty-two second-place finishes. I laughed and said something about that showing how tough this sport really is. "Just imagine if we could get even just half of those races back and figure out how to move up just one spot. Man, I'd already be in the Hall of Fame!" Then I promised that I would be adding to both of those totals, and soon.

The reality was that I was never going to be that close to winning a race again. The dominoes that ultimately pushed me away from the front of the pack started falling the very next weekend.

Sunday, June 12, 2016
Michigan International Speedway

Michigan is a place that has always been very good to me. During the struggles of my first few years at Hendrick Motorsports, Michigan was the racetrack where we twice snapped years-long winless streaks. But it can also be treacherous. It's a two-mile oval with big, sweeping turns that make it super fast. Some of NASCAR's more infamous crashes have happened there. I told you about Dad's broken bones from 1994 that he kept secret while fighting for a championship. That same year, while racing my dad for the title, Ernie Irvan suffered critical head injuries that kept him out of the car for more than a year. Ernie worked hard, came back, and won races again. But in 1999, on the exact fifth anniversary of the crash that nearly killed him, he wrecked again at Michigan, this time in an Xfinity (then Busch) Series practice session. Two weeks later Ernie announced his retirement.

None of that ever caused me to dislike the racetrack at Michigan. Danger is part of the job. Danger showed up for me on lap 62 of the 200-lap race, as I was running three-wide, exiting Turn 2 onto the backstretch. I was running twentieth but jetting through the field and had just cut in between A. J. Allmendinger to my outside and Chris Buescher to my inside. Buescher's car drifted up the track, just slightly, and grazed the left rear corner of my car. If it'd happened a fraction of a second later, I would have already cleared him and been gone. Instead, the tap was enough to smack the rear of my car into the nose of Allmendinger's. I waggled and slapped the wall with the right rear corner of my Chevy and dot-dot-dotted my way down the backstretch wall. Again, it looked like nothing and should have been nothing. My black box recorded it at only 17 Gs. But this was my fourth crash in six weeks. It was far from nothing.

> Slammed wall with right side off turn 2 after contact with the 34. Felt fine driving car back. Felt dinged just a little out of the car when talking to the team. Not buzzed or drunk. Just a visual and mental ding. Got to bus and felt same. Driving to airport and in plane and taxis I felt some dizziness but I feel aware, sharp, not spaced out or drunk.

We were entering an off weekend, which is rare in the Cup Series schedule, so we'd planned a trip back to Germany with some friends. We basically went straight to Europe from the race. That forced me to work overtime, hiding how I felt not only from Amy but our friends too.

Just a wobbly balance issue more than anything. It was certainly a new feeling compared to old similar slight concussions. They are usually a drunk buzz feeling. This is a balance feeling accompanied with lazy and sleepy feeling.

Go back and look through all of the symptoms I'd experienced up to this point. I'd had headaches, I'd felt "unplugged" from my surroundings, and I'd had a ton of anxiety. Lately, I'd suffered from sinus pressures. But balance problems? These weren't little flashes of wobbliness, but a consistent feeling of imbalance. I hadn't been here before.

I felt like I did a good job preparing for the hit at Michigan and that hopefully lessened the potential damage. I think this should clear in 12 to 24 hours.

Later Sunday night. I feel slightly off, not 100% sharp with my eyes on TV but otherwise no issues there. Right eye is sore. Socket and area around eye is sore. Lower temple and area in front of ear is sore. I feel angry for no reason. Doing well biting my tongue but have zero patience.

There was that irritation again.

Still feeling like my issues are balance and mechanical, like buckling a belt or tying a shoe. Even though I feel symptoms it's nothing like usual crashes. Symptoms are different and not as severe.

This was a feeling that was new but was about to become a significant part of my life. Trying to do the simple things that you do every single day but feeling like your brain can't talk to your hands or your feet. Tying my shoes, that always felt like the most glaring problem. I've got my laces in my hands and my brain is like, *C'mon, you know what to do*, but my fingers aren't getting the message. It's like your feet and your shoes are across the room and you can't get to them.

> Monday morning, wake up with aches in my head. Aches are all over and moving from one part of the skull and head to another. Feeling pretty sharp just feel aches and some sadness/emotions.

While we were in Germany, Amy and our friends all noticed that I was disconnected a lot of the time. We had plenty of fun, but I went to bed before everyone else, which is unusual for me. They didn't think it was any indicator of a bigger problem, especially Amy. I had been examined in the infield care center at Michigan and given the okay. I was always worn out after a race, so it wasn't unusual that I'd look like I was dragging a bit, especially when you threw in the jet lag of a trip to Europe on top of that. We also drank more than our share of German beer. The beds were hard. I supposed all of that helped me mask how I really felt, which was scared. I had new symptoms in the balance issues added to the return of my old symptoms.

We returned home the next week and, in my notes, I think you can see that the worrying was starting to wear on me.

> Rest of the week was good.
>   Monday and Tuesday a full week later I'm dealing with headaches around my eye sockets. My eyeballs hurt. Maybe allergies? Constant all day.
>   Sleepy. Lazy.
>   Sad feeling.

Sad? That's not me. I'm a lot of things, but sad isn't one of them. These symptoms made no sense to me and were starting to take a toll because they were so different than anything I had experienced before. In 2012 it felt like someone walking into the room and hitting me upside the head with a baseball bat. This time around, it came on like a slow burn. That's why I thought that maybe it wasn't concussion-related. It really did feel like allergies. Sinus and eye pressure, nagging headaches, and burning and itchy eyes. When I thought back on the crashes I'd had that season, there was no big moment I could connect it back to. The Michigan crash had been a couple of weeks ago, and it wasn't anything special. It was a slap. A broadside wall ding that happens at least a couple of times to somebody in every race.

That's how I reasoned my way through these new feelings, writing them off as allergies. That had to be it. I called Jimmie Johnson, who has always had bad allergies, and he told me, yeah, it sounded like what he was always dealing with in the springtime. I went to my family doctor in Mooresville, North Carolina. He wasn't there, so I saw another guy in the same office, and he agreed with me. I got some allergy medicine and headed west for our first race since Michigan, at the Sonoma Raceway road course in Northern California.

I had a good time, relieved to be back at the track. Behind the wheel of my racecar had become the place where I felt the most normal. The focus it takes, especially the lefts and rights of a road course, kept my mind from constantly analyzing myself. I remember being very conscious of the curbs that are located all over the track, these raised bumpy concrete strips that line most of the course's ten turns. I didn't want to let my tires accidentally wander too far off the asphalt, hit one of those curbs, jar my head, and once again aggravate my symptoms. The day went smoothly, and we finished eleventh.

So the cycle I had been living for years was still intact. Hit something in a race, feel bad for a little bit, be okay by the next race, and cross your fingers that it doesn't happen again. Sometimes the timeline might change a little, the symptoms might last fewer days or they might last a couple of days longer, and the symptoms themselves might change from time to time. Sometimes I would reason my way into some other cause, be it a hangover or jet lag or allergies. But the basic cycle of the experience, it was always the same. I'd be okay by the next weekend, so let's go racing! It wasn't getting any better, but it also wasn't getting a whole lot worse, so I figured that even if it was head-related I must not be doing any real long-term damage.

At the same time, I continued to have my occasional "I think I want to quit" conversations with Kelley and Mike, but nothing would come of it. We'd just move on. We had stuff to do. I had to get to Daytona, where I was the defending champion of the Fourth of July 400-miler.

CHAPTER 6

HARD TRUTHS

Saturday, July 6, 2016
Daytona International Speedway

From the minute I first hit the racetrack for practice, I knew something wasn't right. I'm reluctant to use the word *easy* to describe racing at Daytona, but that place always came easy to me. I would have this constant awareness, knowing where everyone is around me at all times and just instinctively knowing who is going to do what and what's coming next. I can be sitting in a pack of cars and just instantly sense things like, *Okay, the outside line is about to be on the move*, and pull it up there just in time to catch that train and go to the front. When I'm in the draft, I'm calling the shots. Everyone knows it too.

But when practice started, I immediately realized that those abilities were gone. If I made a move, it was a beat too late. If I sensed a guy was going to make a move, by the time I processed that thought, he had already made it and was gone. He had dusted me. It was like everything was moving at seven-eighths' speed.

Racecar drivers don't do anything at seven-eighths' speed. Perhaps I had experienced this symptom before, but never at the racetrack, certainly never in the car.

Another symptom was returning now too. That constant irritation was creeping back. I could feel it. It was like that day at Talladega in 2012, the day of my "bloodthirsty" rant, when I suddenly wasn't able to control my emotions or put a filter between my mind and my mouth. The timing couldn't have been worse.

When I returned to my motorcoach, Amy informed me that Rick Hendrick wanted me to come by his bus for a chat. I knew what he wanted to talk about. My contract with Hendrick Motorsports was up at the end of 2017, the next season. Rick, eager to keep our sponsors happy, wanted us to start talking about getting an extension signed before it became a hot topic in the media. Amy knew I was having a bad day, and she made me promise to keep a cool head. I told her that I would.

Instead, I totally blew up. Rick thought we were going to talk about another three-year deal, but instead what he got was a rant from me, telling him I was tired of driving racecars. I yelled it. I told him I was done, that I hated it. I wasn't having any fun on the racetrack or really anywhere, so I was done. I could leave that bus right then and there and walk out of the track and never come back and that would be fine with me. For accuracy, take those last five sentences and cram a bunch of cuss words into them.

I know he wasn't expecting me to say what I said. Heck, I wasn't expecting to say what I said, either. But my filter was gone. I felt awful. That was it. While I carried on it was like all of a sudden I realized the truth. I had felt awful for months and my brain might be hurt and my future might be in jeopardy and I'd been keeping this a secret from everyone and now I couldn't even get around Daytona worth a flip—and all of that just boiled up right there, right in front of poor Rick.

I wasn't mad at Rick. I didn't hate racing, either. I was just angry. Rick and racing, they just happened to be what was sitting there in my way when that anger finally blew up. What I didn't realize—and neither did Rick—was how sick I really was.

You know how when you get the flu, you don't have time for anyone or anything? You just want to lay there. "Leave me alone; I'm sick." Well, that's how I felt. Because I was sick, and I had been sick for a long time.

This time, though, I felt sick at the track and in my racecar. I guess that's what it finally took for it all to become real to me. As odd as this might sound for you, having just read all of my stories and notes from all the times I didn't feel right over all those months and years, that weekend at Daytona was the first time I really came to grips with the fact that *Dale, something is really wrong with you*.

But you know what? I still raced. We finished twenty-first at Daytona. And except for my meeting with Rick, I must have done a pretty nice job of acting normal. I had a pre-race media session that lasted a half-hour, and you know how many concussion questions I got? Zero. Same for the post-race. The Big One happened on just past the halfway point of the night, and I got jostled around a little but managed to snake my way through the pileup without suffering a big lick. As bad as I already felt, I can't imagine what I would have been like if I'd suffered another big hit that night.

We were full bore toward the next weekend's race at the bumpy Kentucky Speedway, but that whole week I felt terrible. When we made a visit to the Nationwide Children's Hospital in Columbus, Ohio, it exposed a trigger that has continued to varying degrees ever since. This might sound odd coming from a guy who has spent his whole life in crowds, whether it was following my dad around as a kid or making my living in front of thousands every day, but I've never felt comfortable when I'm surrounded. That's particularly true when it's a really over-stimulating environment, like a big event, and even worse when the focus is on me. You'd think I'd be used to that by now, but I'm not.

Now, that kind of situation didn't merely make me nervous or anxious. It taxed my mind to the point that it set off my symptoms so badly that I felt like I needed to grab ahold of something to stay upright. The thought that other people might see that and realize I was struggling only made it worse.

> Still feel wobbly. It gets worse in populated areas or when I'm being fed a lot of information. Went to Children's Hospital and felt very dizzy going through the appearance. I feel worse wearing sunglasses than without. No sinus pain or headache.
>
> Turning around quick or any quick movement makes me lightheaded for a second.

Saturday, July 9, 2016
Kentucky Speedway

The next weekend, I had another new at-track symptom. We were in the garage after a practice session, and I looked up at the scoring pylon to see where everyone had run. The numbers on that pylon were fuzzy, out of focus. I asked my PR rep if it looked fuzzy to her. She said no.

> At track for practice. Have some moments walking around that get me dizzy. Head feels weird, some sinus discomfort

possibly. Blurry vision at 50 or more feet. Eyes feel sore and irritated a little bit.

Felt off balance all weekend. Worse on Friday and Saturday and through the next week.

We finished thirteenth at Kentucky, marking two consecutive races without any additional hits, and now I was nearly a month removed from my last crash, the one at Michigan. But that didn't stop my symptoms from hanging around. Now, they never seemed to take a break. It was seven days a week, and they were getting worse. When I read this now, it kind of feels like all those other notes, starting in April 2014, were leading up to this one.

Dealt with more and more nauseous feelings. Mentally felt sharp. But standing balance was bad and head felt like it was hit with a bat. Just felt in a constant state of daze.

Went to doctor on Tues and Wed. Ruled out everything like allergy or inner ear.

Docs think it's a brain injury.

While the rest of the NASCAR world was preparing to travel to the New Hampshire Motor Speedway for the season's nineteenth race, Amy and I were back at Dr. Jerry Petty's office. We ended up there because I had finally done what I should have done much earlier, at the very least two weeks earlier at Daytona. On Tuesday morning, when I woke up, stood up, and could barely walk straight, I called Rick and I finally confessed to him how bad I'd been feeling. What I proposed was that we should see how I felt by week's end, but to have Alex Bowman ready to jump into my car, just in case.

Rick was not happy with me. He said he wasn't mad at me

because he was my boss. He was mad at me because he was my friend and he didn't want me to suffer. What Rick says now is that he realized something wasn't right with me when I blew up on him in his motorcoach at Daytona, but he didn't realize how bad it really was. Not until I called him with this news.

He told me that I had been stupid to be out there racing while I felt like this, and that, no, he wasn't going to call any substitute drivers yet.

Then he told me to stop screwing around and go see Dr. Petty.

I remember I drove to Dr. Petty's office in Charlotte, and when I got out of the car I had to walk really carefully across the parking lot, hanging on to the rail and the front door. That's how jacked-up my balance was. What started as a small symptom had now grown to the point that any movement that included rotation of my head and eyes, like walking around a corner or up a set of stairs, would trigger a total imbalance, like I was going to fall down.

With that in mind, Dr. Petty took me upstairs and put me through a set of tests designed to identify inner-ear issues that racers can develop, like vertigo and what we've always called *rocks in your ears*. The goal of those tests was to try to re-create the conditions that caused my imbalance, but they couldn't do it. We did another MRI, and I took another ImPACT test. Dr. Petty looked over all the results and knew instantly what the cause was. The scans were fine, and my new ImPACT results lined up very nicely with my last baseline test in 2014, except for one aspect. My visual memory was lagging.

"Dale, you've suffered another concussion. You aren't racing this weekend." He called Rick and told him the same thing.

The notes that I took over that weekend only further emphasize how irresponsible it would have been for me to have tried to drive my car at the next race at New Hampshire Motor Speedway. On

Friday, while Alex Bowman was qualifying the No. 88 in the twenty-sixth starting position, this was me:

> Woke up Friday morning feeling really drunk. Worse than before. Kinda clearing up a little as I get moving but balance is worse than it's been. Got in car at lunch with L.W. and felt very very dizzy and nauseous as I've ever been.
>
> Close to puking. Seems to be getting worse. Cleared up back to original symptoms an hour later and was steady the rest of the day.

On Saturday, while Alex ran twenty-second fastest in the final "Happy Hour" practice session:

> Saturday woke up much like Thursday. No improvement. Slept very late. Had a moment laying down when the room spun perfectly counterclockwise 45 degrees. That was new. It was over as quick as it happened. Balance issues very similar as the past few days as of 1 pm. When I get up I get very wobbly and nauseous. Only feel better laying or sitting. Head feels like it's super heavy when I don't lean it on something. Went to the hospital for a CT scan. Got really wobbly and drunk feeling by all the stimulation of the people and hallways and activity. But my emotion was fun, not anxious.

On Sunday, while Alex finished twentieth in the race, the final car on the lead lap:

> Sunday. Woke up early real wobbly. Even laying down, movement made me feel drunk. This day feels pretty bad, like

Friday. 11 AM I feel terrible. Severe imbalance. Disoriented. Nausea, real close to vomiting. Felt much better later in the evening around 5. So much better. Way tolerable. When I went to get ready for bed at 9 I felt worse. Climbing stairs and walking 100 or more feet really made me drunk and nauseous. I laid in bed and felt better.

You know, it's strange when I think about it now, but when Dr. Petty broke the news to me that I would have to sit out New Hampshire, it wasn't the devastating moment that it had been in 2012, the previous time he'd told me that I had to get out of my racecar. I think part of it is that I was actually a little relieved that we had a diagnosis. It was out in the open now. I didn't have to keep on being so sneaky about it. But I also think that the news was manageable because I believed that I was probably just going to miss one race. I'd sit out New Hampshire, get some rest, do some exercises, and be back for the Brickyard 400 at Indianapolis Motor Speedway the following weekend. That's pretty much how it had gone down in 2012, right?

Tuesday, July 19, 2016
Pittsburgh, Pennsylvania

Like in 2012, we were headed back to Pittsburgh.

Today we get up early and go to see Micky. I felt exactly the same this morning as most other mornings. No nausea getting ready. I sense my balance giving me problems when I'm up and walking but I'm less aware of it. I'm either getting used to it or it is slightly improved.

It's so hard to measure because my vision hasn't changed, but my eyes have a hard time locking onto a moving object. My eyeballs and my inability to operate them properly is frustrating . . . When the plane would turn to ascend or descend it would trip my head out.

When I walked into the UPMC Sports Medicine Concussion Program offices, I was surprised to be back. Dr. Micky Collins, however, says he wasn't super surprised to see me again. He had nailed me and my personality in 2012. I was a worrier. I was prone to anxiety. I internalized a lot of what and how I felt, just as I was internalizing the details of my illness, shared only in my private notes. I tell people all the time that my 2012 accidents had made me feel more susceptible to future injuries, and Micky believed that too.

So here we were, face-to-face once again. We chatted about those four years since our last visit, and we did an inventory. It was scary. I counted up ten incidents that I believed may have resulted in concussions. Ten. There had been five crashes this year alone.

As we had our conversation, we also had an audience. In 2012 it had only been me, Amy, and Dr. Petty in the room. Now the three of us were joined by Kelley; her husband, L.W.; and Mike Davis. My initial consultation with Micky was with that whole group sitting there with us, watching and listening.

The audience aside, the setting and the situation were like déjà vu, like 2012 all over again. But what I couldn't tell was how much more refined the processes had become for Micky and his staff in the four years since I'd been there. Remember when I told you about all those people lined up in his office during my first visit? The UPMC clinic sees 20,000 cases per year. That means they'd had 80,000 patient visits between my first appointment and this one.

Think about how much information had been gathered over that time. In racing, we are constantly discovering new ways to make racecars go faster, using the tiniest changes to the most obscure pieces and parts of the car, stuff we would have never even thought to look at just a few years ago. That's how fast the technology of racing moves. Well, the technology of brain science moves even faster. You can read a book or an article now—and I've read most of them—that was written just a few years ago, and so much of it already feels dated. Just like trying to run a 2012 model racecar in a 2016 race.

Micky immediately recognized that my symptoms were more severe than 2012. Then, it had all been sort of a general fog with only flashes of anxiety, balance, and vision issues. Now, all of that more intense stuff was around all the time. So were my irritable mood swings, nausea, and sensitivity to busy, overwhelming environments. Back in his office I was reminded of his explanation from four years earlier, about the six different types of concussions—cognitive/fatigue, ocular, migraine, cervical, anxiety/mood, and vestibular. There were posters all over the UPMC building explaining those six types and listing the symptoms of each.

It all sounded like what was happening to me. All of it. Had I suffered all six types? Micky reminded me of another lesson he'd taught me in 2012, that the brain's regions and systems didn't exist in separated compartments. They are all interconnected through constant communication. So when there is an injury to one area, it's going to affect the others. It's really not unlike the geometry of a racecar. If we make a chassis adjustment to the right front corner, then that also affects the left rear, the corner connected to it diagonally. Likewise, if one of those corners is damaged and the car is no longer in balance, then that's going to create wear and tear throughout other areas of the car when they are working to compensate for the corner that's no longer keeping up.

Micky explained to me that, like 2012, my primary issues were rooted in my vestibular system, the sensory system that controls our sense of balance and spatial orientation, and uses those to coordinate our movements. That's tied to our eyes. For me, it also tugged on my emotional systems. Why? Because when the vestibular and ocular systems are not working at 100 percent, it leads to increased analysis, anxiety, and worry, especially for a person with my personality.

The term Micky uses is *rumination*. I ruminate. A lot. He realized that in 2012 too. That's why he wasn't so surprised to see me back in the building all those years later.

As Micky sent me off to the gym to be evaluated by the physical therapy team, there was plenty of ruminating going on among the large group who'd made the trip to Pittsburgh with me. While I was being pushed on exercise machines and in front of computer screens to figure out where my new mental and physical limits were, Dr. Petty was in constant contact with Hendrick Motorsports, who was wanting to know as soon as possible what my status was going to be for the Brickyard 400. Meanwhile, Kelley was running our businesses from the lobby of UPMC, all just as anxious to know if the guy whose name was on the building would be racing five days from now. On the other ends of their phone lines were our sponsors.

Don't misunderstand here. No one was calling and screaming, "What's up with Dale? We have to know!" But there are so many parts and pieces and people and scheduling connected to every race weekend, and it's all dependent upon me being there to participate. Some poor sales guy, he's been working for months to do a big deal, and his closing move might be that the CEO gets to chat with me at the Brickyard, but now I might not be there—that guy needs a heads-up. The race team is about to load up our racecar for the weekend, and they need to know what driver is going to be in that car when they hit the track for practice on Friday.

So I understood the concern. And I like to think they were also worried about, you know, me.

While everyone paced the floor of Micky's office, I rode an exercise bike and did rounds on an elliptical machine. I also did what they call dynamic exercises: thirty rounds of deep squats, lunges, and medicine ball rotations, where I would catch a heavy ball, turn to one side or the other, and toss it to a target behind me. I also did functional testing, speed-stepping up and down on a one-step frame, forward/backward jogging, and a jump/turn/toss. After every exercise, measurements were taken, looking to see what symptoms, if anything, had been triggered and how bad they became. What they found was that when dealing with straight horizontal lines—anything that moved horizontally and kept my eyes focused straight ahead—I was okay. But anything that moved off that line, that went vertical and took my eyes into different directions, that's when my mind struggled to keep up.

Looking at Micky's notes from this appointment, it says that on the bike I showed no symptoms, but the elliptical triggered both dizziness and headaches. Squats and lunges? Nothing. But the twisting and turning of those medicine ball rotations registered a six out of ten on the dizziness scale. The speed step drill—quick movements up and down on a little one-step platform—that was the worst. That scored an eight on dizziness and a five on nausea.

After a couple of hours in the gym, Amy and I rejoined the group. Micky came in with the new data in hand. That data didn't tell him that I was concussed; he'd known that as soon as he'd seen me. What it did was put the focus on my specific issues, giving us a target to hit and allowing his staff to design a rehabilitation plan aimed at that target. They call it *exertion therapy*, using exercises to take me right up into my symptom triggers, and then using those same exercises to retrain my mind, eyes, and body how to work together to handle those situations. If an exercise made me feel bad, then I would take that home with me and do it until it no longer made me sick. If an exercise didn't cause any issues, it went off the list.

This time around, my homework included exertion exercises—squats, lunges, "wood chop" catches and tosses of the medicine ball, time on the stationary bike and elliptical machine, and those dang speed step-ups. There was also a list of four finer tasks. There was a backward ball toss, where someone would have to stand behind me as I threw a ball over my shoulder to them, then I would rotate and catch it on the other side, and repeat. I did a "standing static" that on paper looks like nothing—standing on a soft cushion, feet together, and closing my eyes for twenty seconds. All I was supposed to do was stand there. But when I closed my eyes, I would lose my balance and pitch one way or the other. It was the same for my "gait" test, which is basically the same test a police officer gives someone when they've been pulled over for a DUI check. You walk heel-to-toe along a straight line, twenty steps, with your eyes closed. I couldn't even come close. I'd get to the third step and just veer off to the left to the point that I'd have to catch myself.

Micky was very matter-of-fact about my condition. He reiterated the importance of keeping my anxiety level low, toning down those ruminations, and prescribed me a low dose of Klonopin, an anti-anxiety medication, with the hope that it would help me focus on my rehab tasks and not the reason for them.

What he said to me next also helped. It was the same promise he made in 2012: "Dale, we can fix this. This is treatable."

Then, taking the temperature of the room, he reminded me of what the real issue was here. It wasn't the Brickyard 400 or sponsors or schedules. The only schedule that mattered now was the one I had in my hand, the one that listed my daily exercises. He knew I was worried about all of that other stuff, the racing stuff. I was ruminating again. "I don't care about any of that," he told me. "All I care about is making you better and giving you the tools to repair this. Right now, that's what you need to care about too."

Micky told me that he would see me again in two weeks. Everyone in the room looked at their calendars, and they knew what that meant. I would be out of the car not just for Indianapolis but the following weekend at Pocono Raceway too.

Dr. Petty dialed Rick Hendrick. All he said was, "He ain't racing."

CHAPTER 7

BATTLEGROUND
OF THE MIND

July 2016
Dirty Mo Acres, Mooresville, North Carolina

I want to tell you about Amy Earnhardt.

It was the summer of 2016, and at that time she was still Amy Reimann, my fiancée. And because of everything that I was dealing with, it was easy for us to forget that we were also in the middle of planning a wedding, scheduled for New Year's Eve.

As my time out of the racecar was extended, and as rumors about my retirement started getting louder, a lot of people spoke up. They had a very hard time dealing with it all. I'm referring to a not-small percentage of my fans but also to some people who are much closer to me. Some, as close to me as people can get. The thought of me not doing my job . . . well, it made them very emotional and, in a lot of cases, irrational. They looked for something or someone to blame.

So this is for anyone who tried—and might still try—to blame Amy. The people who said stuff like, "Well, she doesn't want him to race, so that's why he's getting out of the car" or "Getting engaged to her has made him soft" or "I bet while the doctors won't let him race, she's at home trying to talk him out of ever coming back."

Do you want to know who was setting the alarm every morning and dragging my miserable butt out of bed to do my exercises? Amy. You want to know who set up my gym in our garage and then went in there every day, putting me through my paces like a personal trainer-turned-drill-sergeant for two or three hours a day? Amy. It was Amy who recorded video of my exercises in case Micky or Dr. Petty needed to see them. It was Amy who stood behind me catching that medicine ball and tossing it back, over and over and over again. Amy put up with my whining and complaining. Amy listened to my rambling hours of self-analysis of how my body and brain were feeling and functioning. Amy took the brunt of my temper tantrums on the days when my condition left me no control over my emotions. Amy drove me everywhere. Amy put her shoulder under me when I lost my balance and she caught me when I fell down.

This is the guy she was living with that July.

Wednesday July 20: real wobbly balance and sight in the morning. Feel like my muscles aren't getting the message from my brain. Haven't started training yet. Will do this evening. Went to hospital for blood work and felt so damn drunk and wobbly. Just incredibly debilitated.

Felt better as we got to noon. Did my exercises. Hard but

got through it. Got Amy on a Bosu ball with feet together and eyes closed and she gets my exact symptoms.

Thursday: Woke up wobbly but not quite as bad. Vision seems to have a 5% to 10% improvement in steadiness at distance. Still bouncy eyes riding in a car. No nausea. Taking the meds. Don't feel the amount of wobbly I had waking up yesterday but it's still very much there. Worked out. Got some headache on the physical stuff. More wobbly with each physical workout.

Around 7 p.m. I got real wobbly and felt slow mentally. Not foggy. Just lazy mentally.

Amy was by my side for everything. She was at every doctor's appointment, from Charlotte to Pittsburgh. Whenever any news was delivered by those doctors she was there to hear it, the first to either celebrate with me over the good news or hold my hand and calm me down for the bad news. When people, including family, didn't understand what was happening and couldn't understand why I didn't just shake it off and get back to the racetrack, it was Amy who had to try and explain to them how bad off I really was. That's a hard conversation, especially when you are explaining it to people who grew up in that "put a washcloth on it" mentality.

You want to know how many times she said, "Dale, I think you need to quit driving racecars"? Zero. Not once. We had conversations about whether or not I should keep driving, but when we did they were started by me. There were a couple of times when I would say I was 90 percent sure I was done as a racecar driver. There were other times when I would put that number closer to 50 percent. On other days it might be 0 percent. No matter what percentage I was sitting on, Amy was going to leave the decision up to me—and she made sure I was doing my exercises, no matter where my head was.

Being the spouse of a racecar driver, even a healthy one, is a tough experience, especially for someone who didn't grow up around racing. But if someone really loves you, then they also appreciate the things that you love. Amy knew from the very beginning that I loved racing. She was never going to be the person to get in the way of that, even during the times when racing didn't love me back.

Friday: Felt like this morning was the best morning physically, with balance and eyes. Saw improvement in rehab. Eye chart, gait test, ball toss.

Saturday and Sunday, more the same. I have a new way to describe what my eyes do. When I move my head left to right, objects move left to right in the opposite direction.

Monday: Not a great day. Went to see TJ Majors and played video games and went to lunch. Really struggling with balance and eyes. So disappointing. The day sucked all around. Went to basketball and eyes went nuts. My reaction time is off, and I'm just not coordinated. Very drunk feeling.

Annoyed at the lack of progress.

Being out of the racecar again was sad, but when I'd been told it would be another couple of weeks, I never felt crushed by that news. It still felt temporary. I figured, okay, I'm missing two more races, so three in total? That's only one more than we missed in 2012, and we'll come back for the road course at Watkins Glen and it'll all be good. Besides, my car was in good hands. I personally pushed for Alex Bowman and they'd given him a shot. In addition, Rick had somehow talked Jeff Gordon into coming out of retirement to run the next two races, the Brickyard 400 and the Pennsylvania 400 at Pocono. Jeff Gordon? That's a pretty insane substitute driver. I was blown away. ("What can I say?" Rick told me later. "I'm a heckuva salesman.")

My team was taken care of. My businesses were taken care of. Everyone told me it was time to take care of myself for a couple of weeks. And again, as scary as being diagnosed with a concussion might be, it felt good to have a goal. Every time I visited the doctors in Pittsburgh, they would fill out two very important lines in their appointment notes: a short-term functional goal and a long-term functional goal. During my rehab, the short-term goals changed. But the long-term goal was always the same: "Return to racing."

The problem was, as is so apparent in my notes, that I wasn't making progress toward that goal nearly as fast as I had in 2012. I knew I was in much worse shape now, but I still believed the recovery time was going to be relatively short. My rehab then had lasted barely a week. Now, entering the second week after my first 2016 appointment with Micky, it was becoming obvious that this was going to take a while.

Tuesday. Awful balance. No good. May be wrong but feel like I may be falling to the left most often. Especially in the gait exercise. Wobbly all day. Played games on my computer.

Wednesday and Thursday very similar days. Better balance but terrible gaze stabilization.

Friday. Balance a little worse as is gaze stabilization than the past couple days. Noticed my energy not as sustainable.

Last several days no changes. Becoming more worried with eye issue not improving. Seeing symptoms get a little worse at night getting tired at 7/8 pm. Ready for bed earlier than normal. Sleeping harder and deeper than normal. Workouts slightly do increase balance issues.

Tuesday, August 2, 2016
Pittsburgh, Pennsylvania

I was back to see Micky, having stuck to my exercise plan and confident that there had been improvement. But now I had a new, growing problem. Okay, it wasn't new, but it was the one aspect of my condition that seemed to be getting worse instead of better. You read it in my notes. My eyes now felt like they had a total inability to stay locked in on an object. I had learned that this is called *gaze stabilization*, and the title accurately describes the problem. Whenever I tried to focus on anything up ahead, especially if I was in motion, my eyeballs would just start bouncing around, like they were on springs, each one doing whatever it wanted all on its own. I had heard other racecar drivers, like ESPN analyst Ricky Craven, describe that kind of sensation after suffering concussions, but it always sounded a little crazy to me. Now I knew exactly what that felt like.

For the vestibular system to properly do its job of helping us maintain balance, making sure our head, eyes, and body are in sync, the communication lines between all of those parts has to be clear. My stretched, bent, and snapped communication lines weren't providing a clear path. Not yet. It would be like going into an airplane and cutting the wires that connect the gyroscopes to your attitude, heading, and turn indicators. More accurately, it's like cutting those wires and then reconnecting them with a shoddy tape job so they keep coming apart and back together. There are short circuits in the systems that are supposed to tell you where you are, where to look, and where the horizon is.

It was particularly terrible whenever I was in a car. I couldn't even look out the window. I'd have to stare into the floorboard to keep my eyeballs from bouncing and my world from spinning out of control. That's a horrible condition for anyone. For a racecar driver, it's just about the scariest scenario you could come up with.

Micky explained that a lot of my fatigue was tied to this issue. The gaze stability center is located in our brain stem, uses a ton of energy, and can become tired very easily. Most people probably think of the brain as this organ that's just sitting there in our skulls, not moving or pumping or anything like that, so it doesn't use as much energy as something like our muscles or hearts. But the reality is that it uses far more energy than any other part of our anatomy. It burns calories. It uses 20 percent of the energy that the body needs, and that's when we're at rest. When you're hurt, and your brain is having to work overtime just to try and do normal everyday tasks, like maintaining balance, it's no wonder exhaustion sets in. Especially if you were already an overthinker like me.

My gaze stabilization problems are why the second half of every Pittsburgh visit was spent with Dr. Nathan Steinhafel at Pediatric & Adult Vision Care. There I was run through a battery of eye tests, the goal being the same as it was at UPMC: to find my limits and give me a list of tasks to complete at home on top of those already given to me by Micky's staff. It was all designed to retrain my eyes to better connect with my brain and function properly. That included updated prescriptions for my glasses, which were like orthopedic shoes for my eyes. They were big and chunky, but I was told to wear them at least 70 percent of the day, and they definitely helped. I was given computer-driven tasks on my laptop that would force my eyes to track moving objects to the point that I felt totally cross-eyed, but I could also feel the strength starting to build back up. I also had a battery of chart-driven eye tests. In one, I would stand ten feet from an eye chart and try to read it top to bottom, but also while turning my head side to side in a "no" motion and then up and down in a "yes" motion. There were a lot of variations on this, all challenging me to rapidly focus, track, and read while in some sort of motion. Man, that's hard enough to do when everything is working right!

So another trip to Pittsburgh, another exertion workout, another pair of glasses, and another long list of exercises to take home. This came with another "we will see you back here in two weeks," which also meant "you still aren't cleared to race."

That meant another call from Dr. Petty to Rick Hendrick and another call from Rick to Jeff Gordon and Alex Bowman. Jeff agreed to run that weekend's race at Watkins Glen, the event I had originally eyed for my comeback. Now I wouldn't be going at all.

Or wait, maybe I was?

Friday, August 5, 2016
Watkins Glen International

If ever there was a time when anxiety was going to cause me to overdo my self-analysis of my symptoms, it was the Friday when I wrote this note:

Aug 4. Getting tired in middle of the day. Want to sleep very badly. Can lay down and sleep for hours. Balance seems to be slightly better. Not as woozy when sitting or standing or rolling in and out of bed. Still there but improved. Eyes not coming along as I would like. When I'm well rested the eyes seem their best. Felt like wearing my glasses bothered my eyes and distance stability more, especially before noon.

The next day I was traveling to upstate New York to make an appearance at Watkins Glen Raceway during the NASCAR Cup Series race weekend. It would be the first I had seen anyone outside of my doctors, closest friends, and immediate family since I'd driven at Kentucky Speedway, one month earlier. It would be a quick up-and-back day trip from North Carolina, with Mike Davis and Hendrick Motorsports VP and general manager Doug Duchardt as my escorts. I wasn't planning to visit with Greg Ives and my crew as they helped Jeff Gordon prepare for Sunday's race. I was really self-conscious of getting in their way, of being a distraction. I had even removed myself from our group text conversations. The real purpose for the trip was to do a media Q&A session.

I don't think I can fully express to you how nervous I was about this visit to the racetrack. Throughout my different concussions and my different fights to battle back over the years, various symptom triggers would come and go, some worse at some times and others worse at other times. But the one constant force that would push me over the edge was being in big, crowded, overstimulating environments.

The entire time I was away from the racetrack in 2016, the biggest challenges for me were whenever I would venture out into the world. I would be doing well with my exercises and thinking I was making a bunch of progress, and then I would go to the grocery store with Amy and it was like a nightmare. I'd walk the aisle of the store and the lights were bright and the aisles would feel narrow and I would have to physically catch myself. I'd feel like I was about to fall over on my face right there in the store. That made me paranoid about the people watching me. People are always watching me anyway, especially around my hometown of Mooresville, North Carolina, but now when they were watching me it would feel like it did at that barbecue place in Kansas City after my big 2012 test crash. It felt like they were judging me all the time, sizing me up. *"I was just reading about all Dale Junior's concussions, and dang, look, he can't even walk straight through the produce aisle!"*

My security blanket was my couch at home. Whether I was stumbling through a workout or freaking out at the grocery store, if I could just get back to my couch, then I knew I would be okay. That was the one place in the world where I could even feel the tiniest bit normal. Only a few people in the world had access to my den—well, them and our dogs. I called it my *charging station*. Like an iPhone, just let me plug in and recharge and get my energy back up.

Now we were headed to the racetrack, maybe the most over-stimulated environment in the world. It's crowded, loud, covered in color, and there's no place on earth where more people are staring at my every move all the time. So why in the world would I go there? Because Micky said I had to. I had my exertion exercises to push my limits at home. Now he stressed the importance of exposure exercises, to push my limits well outside the comfort zone of the house. He said it was particularly important for me to get back into my regular work environment, to remind my brain of how it operated in the garage area. People who suffer physical injuries, they have to reteach their healing parts how to do the jobs those parts used to take for granted. I had to do that with my brain.

Doug and Mike both remember that I was very quiet on the trip up to the Glen, even more than usual. It took about a half-hour to ride from the airport to the track, and during that time I finally spoke up. I told them they really needed to keep an eye on me. I was worried how I was going to look in front of the national media for the first time, and then how I might look to the fans watching at home. All those worries that kept me from revealing my first concussions were the same reason I was worried now. I remembered how people reacted to Ernie Irvan, Steve Park, and Ricky Craven when they'd returned from head injuries. They had all suffered from the same eye issues I had now, but that was years earlier and none of them had received the kind of advanced treatment that I was getting from Pittsburgh. They had "lazy"-looking eyes and slightly slurred speech. Even after Ernie and Steve came back to win races at NASCAR's highest level, they were still given the "damaged goods" treatment. I was worried I might not be able to recall a word or maybe I would talk a little slower than I had before. It was hard for me to see the differences in me now versus me earlier in the summer, but these folks who hadn't seen me since then, they'd notice anything different and they'd notice it quickly.

Honestly, I was just worried that I was going to lose my balance and fall down trying to walk up to the front of the media center with all those cameras rolling.

I didn't. All things considered, I thought I handled the thirty-minute press conference pretty well. I was asked about the work I was doing to return. "Racecar drivers don't have much patience to begin with . . . so it's frustrating . . . We're just taking it one appointment at a time." I was asked what I'd learned during my time away and I admitted that I'd made a mistake multiple times by hiding how I felt. I also admitted that if I was twenty-one years old instead of forty-one, I might still be tempted to ignore concussion symptoms and keep racing, but I wanted the young guys to know that was the wrong move. I confessed that my rehabilitation was taking much longer than I had expected. I also confessed that I was still confused as to how all of this had even happened, with no single giant origin hit to trace it back to like we could to the Kansas tire test in 2012.

I think that for the fans who were watching, maybe they were hoping for a bunch of ironclad answers like, "This is what happened and I'm back to this percentage of being okay and I will be back for this race on this date!" That's not what they got. But I was as honest as I possibly could have been.

Mostly, I was asked about when I thought I would return and if I thought there was a chance that I might not return. Nate Ryan, then with *USA Today* (now my coworker at NBC Sports), mentioned my career accomplishments and all my good fortune in the sport and wondered if that might be something I had weighed at all, you know, about "it," "a decision," "if it came to that."

I looked at him, smiled, and said, "What?" I paused, kept smiling, and added, "You didn't say the word."

Racecar drivers call it *the r-word*, as in *retirement*. I said that I had every intent of honoring the remainder of my contract with Hendrick Motorsports, through the end of 2017, and I explained that I had already had a conversation with Rick about an extension. I left out the "I want to quit" part.

I was asked if I'd had that r-word conversation with Amy or others during my month on the sidelines. I answered flatly: "No. My doctor thinks that to get through the therapy and get through the symptoms, you don't need to be adding stress to your life. Stress slows down the process. So going into those conversations isn't even necessary at this particular point. The point right now is just to get healthy. To get right. I'm not thinking about the what-ifs. I'm listening to my doctors . . . we went into this with the intention of getting back into the car if I get cleared and I think that's a possibility and so do my doctors.

"As Rick likes to say, I've got unfinished business. I'm not ready to stop racing. I'm not ready to quit."

I might not have been thinking about the what-ifs yet, but to me it was now clearer than ever that everyone else sure seemed to be thinking about them. That press conference wore me out, as did something that I added to the agenda at the last minute, but it was totally worth it. We weren't originally scheduled to make an appearance in the garage, but since I was there I insisted on it. There was no way I was going to be at the racetrack and not go see my guys on the No. 88 Chevy.

I missed them. I already knew that I did, but being there that day reminded me of what I really missed by being out of my car. It wasn't going fast or racing, or really anything about the actual racecar. It was about seeing my guys. That had been taken away from me, and now I knew how much it truly meant to me.

The Watkins Glen garage layout is a bit funky, certainly a lot different than the standard ovals, so we did a lot of walking through gates and crowds and even up and down some hills. The fans went a little crazy in a couple of spots. Micky wanted me to get some max exposure therapy, right? Well, this was it. Seeing the team was so great, but after a few minutes I was ready to go. They needed to get back to work, and I needed to get back home to do my own work.

Aug 6: Went to the racetrack yesterday. Did media. The garage brought out a terrible drunk feeling. It calmed down some on the way home. Woke up this morning with real bad balance. Eyes are working more poorly than normal.

The next two and a half weeks brought some great highs and some big lows. The new exercises added to my to-do list were much more intense. I realized that was a sign of forward progress. My symptoms had been pushed farther out and we had to keep pushing me physically to keep chasing those symptoms and aggravating them. Amy and I went to our house in Key West for a few days. During the day I did my exercises. In the evening we made a point to go out and interact with the crowds. Both felt good.

> Aug 11–14 in Key West. Had a great time. Normal symptoms. No increased issues in busy places. No major changes or problems.

I brought those good feelings home. They didn't last.

> Aug 16 went to JRM and to eat out with Amy. Symptoms increased more than I expected. Balance and eyes struggled with any change in environment.

It's starting to feel like a broken record, isn't it? Imagine living it. As I'd told the media at Watkins Glen three weeks earlier, improvement wasn't coming as fast as I wanted. As great as it had been to see everyone at the track, now they felt a million miles away. It was just me and Amy again in the garage-turned-gym. Part of my prescribed activities now included playing basketball. But even that was supposed to be alone.

I didn't hear much from current drivers. I might not have heard from any of them, save for a few text messages. As odd as this might sound, that doesn't bother me. I honestly can't remember the last time I called a driver to check in on him when he was out of his car with injuries. It sounds cold, but it's just not really in our nature. It doesn't mean you aren't worried about them, but the NASCAR season is the longest season in professional sports. When you're in the middle of it, you're just getting from one race to the next with a schedule full of obligations in between. Someone who isn't on that train is out of sight, out of mind.

I would hear from Kelley. She was hearing from Rick and other people at Hendrick Motorsports. They were all hearing from sponsors. No one wanted to be pushy, but they were hoping for a solid timeline for my return. It's like dominoes falling. The first one is just a nudge. "How's he feeling?" But by the time you get a few nudges going, one hits another and another and the one that hits you, it's not a nudge at all. Kelley often found herself that last domino, the one that hit me, and that led to some pretty heated conversations. It wasn't her fault, but man, we did some arguing a couple of times during all of this.

There was one day in particular when it was me, Kelley, Amy, and L.W. in the den at our house during one of my lower points of the recovery. I tried to explain to Kelley how I was feeling and how I was wrestling with whether or not to come back to racing and I needed her advice. What did she think I should do? Well, she would automatically go into business manager mode. *If you stop now, you will be leaving this much money on the table . . . your retirement portfolio would look like this . . . your relationship with this sponsor would look like this.* I told her that I didn't want my business manager's opinion; I wanted to know what my sister thought. She struggled with that request. Wasn't she worried about my health? Wasn't she worried about what might happen to me if I got into another big crash? Of course she was worried about those things, but it was hard for her to express that. So we did a lot of yelling that day. Like, all over the house.

Kelley remembers that argument well. When she talks about it she shakes her head, smiles, and says, "Keep in mind, now, we are Earnhardts, the children of the Intimidator. Backing down during an argument, that's not really in our DNA." Our whole lives, she's had to strike an impossible balance, taking care of me on a lot of different levels. I already told you, this is the girl who enrolled in military school just so she could look after me. She knows that sometimes it takes her a minute to move from one role to the other, from business manager to sister, but she does it. Asking her to take off one hat for the other, I know that's a big ask, but I had to know what my sister felt. She admits that maybe business manager mode helped her avoid the emotions of sister mode, but eventually sister emerged. Naturally, she wanted what was best for me and my health; she just needed to understand it all better. I think that taking her to some of my appointments with Micky helped with that.

But know this. Even when we argued, I never questioned Kelley's intentions. I never have.

You know which drivers did call me? The retired ones. Guys who had suffered head injuries and wanted me to know I wasn't alone. I also heard from a lot of other guys who said they had suffered concussions, kept them secret, and were now worried about the long-term impact of their stubbornness. I gave them all the phone number of Dr. Micky Collins.

At my most frustrating low points—and there were so many during the summer of 2016—I would call Micky. When he'd given me his personal cell phone number back in 2012 and told me to call him anytime, I told him he might regret that. I wasn't joking. But neither was he. Whenever I called, no matter what time of day or night, Micky answered. If I needed to talk for an hour, he'd listen for an hour. I would tell him about every headache, panic attack, and stumble, and he'd tell me why it was happening and assure me that if I kept doing what he'd told me to then one day it would stop.

If I called him right now and needed to talk for an hour, he'd still listen. And I do. Since the first time I shook hands with him on October 26, 2012, he has been there for me. I will never forget that.

Wednesday, August 24, 2016
Pittsburgh, Pennsylvania

When I returned to see Micky in person for our third 2016 appointment, I knew it had the potential to not be a great examination. There was no question that I had improved pretty dramatically when it came to my symptoms. Only a few weeks earlier I had still been having nausea and dizziness even when I was at rest. Now, even when they really put me through my paces in the UPMC gym, it was becoming more difficult to trigger a lot of that. That was good.

But the problems with my eyes were still pretty bad. During what they call Vestibular/Ocular Motor Screening, or VOMS, Micky and his staff would put me through a series of activities where I would have to track an object with my eyes, and while I did that they would closely monitor the actions of my eyeballs.

They want to see smooth movements, not jerky or staggered jumps, as a patient's eyes track a moving object, or a stationary object while the patient is in motion. They have what they call *smooth pursuit*, which is exactly what it sounds like. How smoothly do your eyes pursue what they are focused on? There's saccadic movement, which is basically your eyes moving around to take in all that is included in the view before them. Watch someone's eyes as they watch a movie or TV. They don't stay fixed on one spot, do they? They move around, looking at every corner of the screen and adding it all up to create the full picture. Doctors watched my eyes to see how well they did that, both horizontally and vertically.

We did Vestibular-Ocular Reflex testing, or VOR, which measures how well your head, eyes, and inner ear work together. This is your body's gyroscope. When you move your head left or right like you're saying no, your eyes compensate by instinctively turning left or right to counter your head movements and stay focused on what's in front of you. This is what I was working on during the exercises when I would move my head and eyes around while walking, all while reading an eye chart taped to the wall in front of me.

The good news was that none of what we did was causing any big dizziness. The bad news is that my eyes still weren't working in tandem like they should. In Micky's notes from this visit the term used was *accommodation insufficiency*. What that meant was that my eyes were still having difficulty focusing. My afternoon visit to see Dr. Steinhafel only underlined my focus issues. He gave me a new pair of chunky glasses to help with my *latent hyperopia*. Basically put, it's farsightedness that can be masked. Your eyes know something is wrong and they figure out a way to work around it. It creates a tremendous amount of strain and you don't even realize it. My eyes needed a rest.

My take-home workout plan now included a much longer list of eye-specific tests. There would be even more walking and tossing and shaking of the head, all while focusing on specific targets. But now the doctors started adding a new ingredient to the recipe: darkness. I was to start walking the hills of my property on various surfaces and I was to do it at dusk, as the light started changing from day to night. I was also to do some of my gym exercises in the dark, eventually mixing in some overstimulation by way of a disco ball. Seriously. It would be just another step in pushing my brain and eyes to have to process a lot of information and eventually work normally under those conditions. I was also to stop playing basketball alone, and start inviting my friends back for some three-on-three, though it had to be non-contact. I was also supposed to continue to ramp up my exposure to crowded public settings.

Amy and I would do my workout in the mornings and then find places to go in the evening, whether it be the race shop, a restaurant, or a Walmart, wherever I was exposed to big crowds, bright lights, and noise. Doug Duchardt had been all over me to start attending our big Tuesday debrief meetings at Hendrick Motorsports, when all four race teams sit and discuss what happened at the last race and make plans for the next one. I'd always felt like that might be weird, seeing as how I'd be the only guy in the room who hadn't actually raced. But now I would be going as part of my exposure therapy.

In the weeks leading up to this visit, I had been starting to drive around a little during the day, but not much. Now they wanted me to start driving more. But only my street car. No racecars. The medical record from August 24 reads: "At this time, Dale does not meet criteria to return to racing given the results of his vestibular, exertion, and vision evaluations and the fact that medication has not reached therapeutic effectiveness."

Zoloft had been added to my meds, the goal being to "continue to dial down the part of Dale's brain that focuses on his symptoms." In other words, my anxiety was again hampering my forward progress. Micky telling me that I still wasn't cleared and that our follow-up appointment would be in a month didn't help that anxiety. Another month? So late September, at best? When the NASCAR postseason would have already started? I think, deep down, I knew that was coming. I wasn't surprised by it. But the reality of adding it all up, that was still not any fun.

Micky sensed anxiety building up in me and quickly worked to calm me down. He told me that he was really encouraged by the progress I was making and, yes, he knew that I was getting frustrated by the pace of it all, but that I was doing much better than I realized. But there was also a hard conversation that I needed to have about that long-term goal of "return to racing" and pausing to think about that phrase *long-term goal*. The stress of trying to shorten my return deadline as much as possible was hampering my progress by throwing gasoline onto my anxiety levels.

Micky told me that as bad as I thought my situation was, it wasn't really. Before he came into my exam room he had been with a professional football player who'd just signed a huge contract. Micky had to tell him that because of his concussions he was going to have to retire. He would never again get to play the game he loved.

"That's not the situation you are in, Dale. We can fix this. We are fixing this." He reminded me that our goals for me were much higher than they were for most. "If our goal was to just get you back to a normal level of brain function, then we'd be close to done already. But we aren't working to get you here . . ." He used his hand to place a mark in the air. "We are working to get you here . . ." He raised his hand above his head. "We aren't working to get you to regular guy level. We are working to get you to racecar driver, elite athlete level. You are doing everything you need to do. But that goal is going to take more time. We need all the time we can get."

I wouldn't be driving racecars again in 2016.

Family photo

Grandson to Ironheart, son to Ironhead. They call me Hammerhead.

Family photo

Dale Earnhardt and his trusty deputy, taking care of business.

Family photo

Me as an undersized eighth grader at Oak Ridge Military Academy.

Family photo

Getting ready to race my late model in 1993 at age eighteen.

Don Hunter/Smyle Media

Don Hunter/Smyle Media

My granddaddy, Ralph Earnhardt, lived by this motto: "Go or blow."

No tougher person to pass, none more intimidating to see in your mirror. That was Dale Earnhardt.

Family photo

Third-generation racers: me; my brother, Kerry; and my sister, Kelley, in 1994.

Dr. Jerry Petty, shown here in 2012 after my crash at Talladega sidelined me for two races.

Tami Pope/Harold Hinson Photography

Harold Hinson/Harold Hinson Photography

The boss of JR Motorsports . . . and her brother. Kelley Earnhardt Miller is always on my side.

Harold Hinson/Harold Hinson Photography

Rick Hendrick and I share a laugh on April 25, 2017, the day I announced my decision to retire.

John Harrelson/Nigel Kinrade Photography

Christa L. Thomas/Harold Hinson Photography

The highs of 2014 were incredible. Here, Amy and I celebrate my second Daytona 500 victory.

The No. 88 team surrounds my car in jubilation after winning at historic Martinsville Speedway.

John Harrelson/Nigel Kinrade Photography

Celebrating one of two victories at Pocono Raceway in 2014.

Steve Letarte and me at Texas Motor Speedway, where I began feeling a return of concussion symptoms.

Nigel Kinrade/Nigel Kinrade Photography

Tom Copeland/Harold Hinson Photography

Not only did my 2016 not end well, but it didn't start well.
This wreck led to an early exit in the Daytona 500.

Harold Hinson/Harold Hinson Photography

A flattened car at Kansas, this one
just two years after a concussion-
inducing test crash there.

The all-too-familiar fog
of concussion returned
in 2014 after this fiery
crash at Texas on lap 12.

Matthew T. Thacker/Nigel Kinrade Photography

Andrew Coppley/Harold Hinson Photography

The hit on June 12, 2016,
at Michigan wasn't huge,
but it sidelined me the
second half of the season.

Nigel Kinrade/Nigel Kinrade Photography

Little did Greg Ives and I know at the time, but this race at Kentucky would be my last of 2016.

Logan Whitton/Nigel Kinrade Photography

Jeff Gordon came out of retirement to drive my car in select races in 2016.

Nigel Kinrade/Nigel Kinrade Photography

Dr. Micky Collins at Darlington Raceway explaining the decision to hold me out the remainder of the season.

Adam Jordan

My team and I pose for a team photo at Darlington Raceway after I was cleared to race at a December test session.

My final Cup race on November 17, 2017, at Homestead-Miami Speedway. It provided me moments with fans . . .

John Harrelson/Nigel Kinrade Photography

Harold Hinson/Harold Hinson Photography

With my boss, mentor, and friend, Rick Hendrick . . .

With my colleagues and fellow competitors . . .

Gary Eller/Harold Hinson Photography

David Tulis/Harold Hinson Photography

And with Greg Ives and the 88 team.

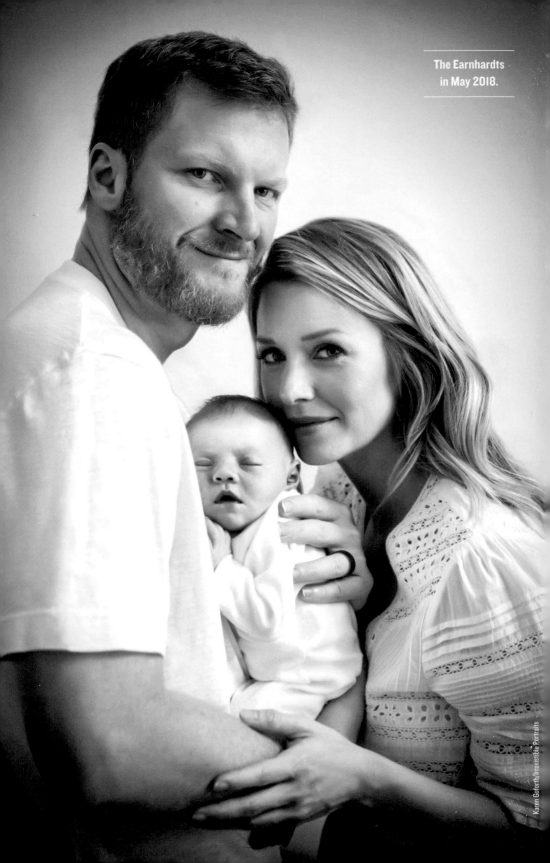

The Earnhardts
in May 2018.

Karen Goforth/Irresistible Portraits

CHAPTER 8

TO RACE OR
NOT TO RACE

Walking to the elevator to leave Micky's office that day, the strangest thing happened. I cried. I wasn't weeping or anything, but I did shed a tear or two. I had Dr. Petty, Kelley, L.W., Mike Davis, and Amy with me. Both Mike and Amy were taken aback that I was getting so emotional. Mike says that he rewound through all the years we had worked together and even before then just watching me on TV, going all the way back to when my father died, and he couldn't remember a single instance of seeing me cry. Amy reacted the same way. She had certainly seen me emotional before, but she wondered aloud why I was crying.

I think the finality of the decision had a lot to do with it. But I also think it just proved that getting out of the car for the remainder of the season was the right thing to do. I could finally release a little bit of that stress and emotion around the whole mess, which had now been going on for so long. During that time, all the way back to 2012, I was always so focused on the rehab work or the coverups of how bad I felt that I hadn't really ever allowed myself to go on and deal with the reality of it. Now I did.

The sadness didn't last long. We had to get back to work. And we had to let the world know I was out for the rest of the year. While we mapped out exactly how to do that, I wrote what ended up being the final note I would enter into my iPhone in 2016. I sound like a man who is relieved to be fully focused.

Eyes see first improvement. Aug 30 2016.

Sunday, September 4, 2016
Darlington Raceway

On September 1, the Thursday before Labor Day weekend, we sent out a press release that read: "Dale Earnhardt Jr., driver of the No. 88 Chevrolet SS for Hendrick Motorsports, has not been medically cleared to compete for the remainder of the 2016 NASCAR Sprint Cup Series season as he continues to recover from a concussion." It went on to lay out the remaining twelve races and how they would be split up between Gordon and Bowman. In the end, I would miss eighteen races in 2016, half the season.

On Saturday afternoon, a few hours before the green flag dropped on the Southern 500, I made an appearance in the Darlington Raceway media center to answer questions about that announcement and was joined onstage with Rick Hendrick and a special guest. Micky came down from Pittsburgh.

I was so glad he was there. I had invited him personally for a number of reasons. First, I just wanted people to see him, to know who he was. Second, I had watched the press conferences held by Sidney Crosby, the great Pittsburgh Penguin hockey player, when he addressed his concussion issues, and he always had doctors at his side, including Micky at one point. When we made our announcement in 2012, I'd had Dr. Petty with me. Third, I knew Rick and I were going to be hit with specific questions about concussions and brain science, and we didn't need to try to answer those. Finally, and this was the most important, I wanted Micky to have the platform and the stage that I knew this press conference would give him. I knew that this was going to be a big deal, that it would be carried live by ESPN, FOX, NBC, and others. There would be people watching who were suffering like me, a lot of them probably keeping it a secret like I had. This was a chance for Micky to reach out to them and reassure them like he had done for me. They could get help and get themselves fixed up. They just needed to know that.

The room was packed. The Southern 500 is one of auto racing's biggest events. In recent years they've turned it into a NASCAR Throwback weekend, when everyone runs classic paint schemes on their racecars and so many people dress up in old uniforms it looks like a NASCAR Halloween party. The theme for this race was the 1970s, right down my alley. Among the audience at my press conference was Barry Williams, aka Greg Brady from *The Brady Bunch*, there to sing the national anthem.

I should have been really nervous—and I suppose I was—but whatever anxiety I had at Darlington paled in comparison to how I'd felt at Watkins Glen just one month earlier. My symptoms were better, but so was my confidence in a big, crowded setting. At Watkins Glen I had been careful to set aside my thick "Wild Thing"–looking glasses. On this day I kept them on for the entire half-hour press conference, even though they made my eyes look kind of huge.

Micky was great. I knew he would be. He started off by giving a quick lesson on concussions. He explained that when the brain is moved around violently inside the skull it creates chemical changes inside the neurons and the cells of the brain, and those changes create "an energy crisis for those cells." He explained the six different concussion types and told the nation that when he'd met with me I had experienced three of those: vestibular, ocular, and anxiety/mood. He explained the idea of specifically targeted treatment plans, and he bragged on me for sticking to that plan.

"When I first saw Dale my goal was to help him become a human being again. I can tell you with confidence that is happening right in front of our very eyes. He is feeling better. He can tolerate a lot more. He's having fewer and fewer symptoms . . . The second goal is Dale becoming a racecar driver again. And yes, we will be working on that as well. I am very confident that we are moving in the right direction in that respect."

He explained that my results, while improving, weren't close to being normal yet. He reiterated the dangers of stress hampering the healing process and said it was no coincidence that, once the decision had been made to not return to racing during the remainder of 2016, my progress had started moving at a much quicker pace than it had while we were going week-to-week on the decision to approve or not approve my return to the racetrack.

Twice he was asked if my previous injuries made me susceptible to concussion going forward, if me getting back into a racecar one day was really that great of an idea. "The only time you run into problems with concussions is when they aren't managed properly. That's what we're doing with this one (managing it properly). We're taking the time that we need. We're doing the treatments that are needed. And that's why we are doing that, with the goal of Dale being able to withstand the biomechanical forces, so that any incidences would not produce a return of difficulties."

The whole time Micky talked, I was grinning. I couldn't help it. I was so glad he was there. I think people could see why I had the confidence in him that I did. The kind of confidence that, when I was asked again about retirement, I could say what I did. "We went through this process in 2012. It was very scary and difficult. Micky told me that I would one day be well and I would win races again. He was right. We got well and I had some of the greatest years and greatest experiences of my career. He's telling me that we can do that again. And I believe it."

We went into the Darlington garage and I got to see my guys and Jeff Gordon again. The fans were great. Micky got to meet some folks too. It really was pretty stunning how much easier it was without the "Will he be back next week?" question dominating everything everywhere I went. I walked that garage with confidence. It had been a while.

During our time there we were asked by both ESPN and Goodyear if I would be the celebrity picker for *College Gameday* the next weekend, when Tennessee and Virginia Tech played a college football game in the infield of Bristol Motor Speedway. ESPN even wanted me to narrate their big movie trailer–style open for their broadcast of the game that night on ABC. They had actually approached me about all that a couple of weeks earlier. I wasn't ready then. I was now.

I was ready for a lot of things now, including a lot of unexpected battles as my rehabilitation plowed into the fall. Throughout September and October, I had more highs than lows. But the lows were still there. My specific instructions from Micky and his staff called for me to go and do things, "normal" things like travel, dinner, concerts, and outdoor activities. I found myself still wrestling with a lot of guilt about that, especially whenever I would think about Kelley and everyone at JR Motorsports or Rick, Greg Ives, and all my guys at Hendrick Motorsports. They were working so hard all the time, still taking care of their normal business and I would think, *What am I doing? Taking hikes and going out to dinner?* I knew there was a lot more to it than that, but I still felt guilty about it. I felt like I was already retired, and I didn't like that.

It didn't help that from time to time I would hear from people doubting what I was doing. Amy and I might post a picture on social media of us having lunch in the treehouse on our property (it's a really nice treehouse) and someone who works for me would see it and soon I'd get a text or a call. "Dude, are you just hanging out in the treehouse? Shouldn't you be doing rehab stuff? Are you not taking this seriously?!" They had no idea I had worked out for hours that morning or that climbing up into the treehouse was actually part of my exposure rehab, that heights had been one of my biggest symptom triggers. Just getting up there and not flipping out, that was a rehabilitation victory.

I had never been a big concert person because of my dislike of big crowds, but Amy and I started going to see shows because we never had before. But we learned not to make a big deal out of it because we didn't want to have to answer to "If you're well enough to fly to Milwaukee for a concert, aren't you well enough to get back into the racecar?!"

There were also calls from some very high-profile professional athletes that were disguised as encouragement but were really sales pitches. I don't have to tell you that the medical industry is big business, but you might be surprised at what other doctors will do to try to grow that business, especially when you're a well-known athlete dealing with a headline-making issue like concussions. They try to lure big patients away from other doctors, and that's what was happening here, asking their sports star clients to do their dirty work. "Dale, I saw your press conference with Dr. Collins and I know you think he's great, but my guy says Micky's treatment methods are all wrong. You should come see my guy." I politely said no.

My guilt extended from worrying that I wasn't doing enough now all the way back to worrying about what I had done—or should have done—before. I unfairly beat myself up putting myself into my current position. As I'd told everyone at Watkins Glen, I didn't let myself think about what-ifs when it came to the future. But I sure did a lot of thinking about the what-ifs of the past.

What if we had said no to that tire test invitation at Kansas in 2012? What if I had come in one lap earlier instead of running the last lap of that twenty-five-lap run so hard? What if that tire hadn't blown? What if I hadn't been so Hammerheaded and told someone how sick I felt as soon as it happened instead of keeping it secret in 2012 and 2016? I would even reach so far back as, hey, what if I had taken better care of myself when I was younger? What if I had gotten way more sleep and drank way less beer in my twenties? Would that have helped me recover faster now?

I told you, my mind never stops. I just have to try to hit the brakes when it starts going too far down one road and then try to steer it down some other one. That's what I tried to learn here, to take that energy and focus it into something more productive than worrying. Like my rehab workouts or planning our wedding.

I learned to shorten up my goals. Instead of allowing that "return to racing" goal to cast a shadow over everything I did, my targets became more short range. Stuff like "go to the grocery store by myself" or "be in good enough shape to go hunting when deer season opens."

We own a hunting camp in Ohio. When the leaves start changing colors, that's where I like to go. In October my friend and fellow racer Martin Truex Jr. made that trip with me and my brother-in-law, L.W. I'm proud to say that I had a big hand in Martin getting his big break in NASCAR. We put him in our Xfinity (then Busch) Series car in 2003, and he's had an incredible career in racing. When we made the trip to Ohio together, he was finishing off a four-win season and setting the stage for a championship run in 2017. Martin is one of my best friends. A big reason for that is that despite all his success he hasn't changed one bit, even now, at the top of his game.

One morning at the hunting camp I was in the garage next to the cabin, doing my exercises. Martin walked in to watch, and it dawned on me that he was really the first racecar driver to watch me do them in person. I was doing the gait test. That's the one that looks and feels like the one you see people doing for police at sobriety checkpoints, walking heel-to-toe for twenty steps along a straight line with your eyes closed. To me, this test was always one of the truest measuring sticks of how I was progressing. In the beginning, I couldn't do one step without losing my balance and pitching completely out to one side. Now I could make it to the end of the line, but sometimes it took a real big effort, my hands flailing like I was a tightrope walker in the circus. A drunk tightrope walker.

I told Martin he should try it. He blasted down that line like it was totally nothing. Then he did it again. I thought about my talks with Micky when he'd raise the bar of our goals with his hand. I thought to myself, *Okay, Dale, you might be close to "normal life" on this thing, but you've still a little way to go to reach "elite athlete."*

I also saw the look in Martin's eyes. He was in disbelief at how I was laboring and couldn't even imagine what it must have looked like weeks earlier, as I described me stumbling around after one step. The look of confusion and then understanding made me wish I could've shown everyone what he'd just seen. *"Man, Dale must have really been messed up."*

Yes, I had been. But I was getting better. I was close and I knew it. Now I was headed back to Pittsburgh to prove it.

Tuesday, November 15, 2016
Pittsburgh, Pennsylvania

My sixth visit to UPMC, and the fifth of 2016, felt different than all the others from the moment we hit the front door. I'd been sleeping better, and it had been a month since I'd had any significant headaches or dizzy spells. Micky had promised that the stress of not having to keep pushing back my imaginary comeback date would be liberating, and it was. With that anxiety reduced, I could feel my rehab improvements happening in relatively big moves instead of baby steps.

As my mental and physical confidence returned, so did my willingness to reconnect with people. I took the crew out for lunch, I rejoined the team's group text, and Amy and I went out socially with Greg Ives and his wife. One night we went to the Cabarrus County Fair and watched the pig races. We even tried some spinny carnival rides, and they didn't make me sick.

Our routine during these visits with Micky had become just that: routine. I met with him and then hit the gym and did tests for exertion, sensory organization, and gaze stability. I had my consultation to talk about my meds. I was off that Klonopin now, and that was fine by me. I could feel my edge returning. Then I headed back up to his office for my post-exam review.

When I got to Micky's office, he had my chart in his hand, and he was smiling. The page that listed the results of my tests in the gym listed a dozen ratings, six taken before the workout and the same six after. Every symptom listed—headache, dizziness, light-headedness, fogginess, nausea, fatigue—was rated at zero out of ten on the scale. "Assessment: No symptoms with exertion." Another page listed goal achievements, everything from levels of balance and stability to functional goals, both short term and long term. Each of those lines now ended with the most beautiful two words you'll ever read: "Goal met."

At the top of his notes, Micky wrote: "With these findings, it is my opinion the patient is asymptomatic from the cerebral concussion he sustained June 2016 and meets criteria for progression towards returning to automotive racing activities."

I wasn't completely cleared. I was to continue my exercises through at least the end of the calendar year. And like 2012, I would have to be put through my paces on the racetrack to see how I reacted to driving a racecar. But this exam was always the biggest hurdle. This time, as I left Micky's office I didn't cry, but there was no shortage of emotion, either. It was the happiest I had been since, geez, I couldn't remember when.

It had been 130 days, a whole four months since I had been behind the wheel of a racecar. With Micky's approval, I would run that total up to 157 days and no further.

During those 27 days between seeing Micky and the test session that would hopefully provide that final clearance, I stayed super busy. I went to the NASCAR season finale weekend at Homestead-Miami Speedway to watch our JR Motorsports drivers Elliott Sadler and Justin Allgaier finish second and third in the final 2016 Xfinity Series championship standings. I went to the NASCAR Champions Week celebration in Las Vegas to accept my fourteenth consecutive

Most Popular Driver Award, voted on by the NASCAR fans. To win that again despite having missed half the season was pretty amazing. I was also a frequent visitor to the Hendrick Motorsports digital simulator, running virtual laps under the watchful eye of Greg Ives, prepping for the most important test session of my life.

Wednesday, December 7, 2016
Darlington Raceway

The helicopter landed early in the morning right next to our house at Dirty Mo Acres. I was wired, but tired. I barely slept the night before because I was so excited to get back into my car.

Anytime the helicopter comes to pick me up the biggest question is, where are the buffalo? I have four buffalo I keep on the property that move between two big sections of fenced-in land on either side of the house. If the helicopter comes whomping in and the buffalo are on the upper section near the helipad, they freak out. So there are windows of time when it can land and when it can't. On this morning the buffalo were in the right place, but they'd be on the move soon, so our departure window to get to Darlington, South Carolina, was tight.

I was ready. Amy was not. I waited as long as I could, but we had to get out of there if we were going to make it to the racetrack on time. It ended up we had to take off without her. I didn't like that because I always wanted her by my side, especially during moments like this morning's test session. She also always wanted to be there for me. But today she simply didn't make it.

The official reason she wasn't ready in time was that the buffalo migration compressed the schedule too much. That's what we said at the time. It was even reported that way in the media. But really, it was because she purposely wasn't trying to get ready on time. All of that work we had done together, she always knew that the goal was to get to this day, to get back in the racecar. She never questioned that. Now that it was finally happening, she needed to stay home and deal with it in her own way. She was going to be in the house, on the safe place of the couch, praying and waiting on text updates from me.

When we got to the racetrack, I wasted no time. I suited up and headed straight for the No. 88 Chevy that was waiting for me in that awesome old carport-looking Darlington Raceway garage. It was a bit of a gray, cold day, but I didn't care. My entire crew had made the trip down, and so had Alex Bowman, which I thought was pretty dang cool of him to do. Dr. Jerry Petty was also there. Just like my comeback test at Gresham Raceway Park in 2012, Dr. Petty would be there to administer a handful of quick field tests to see how my mind and eyes were reacting to being back in a racecar. Once I was up to speed, I'd be traveling upwards of 180 mph around NASCAR's quirkiest speedway, a 1.366-mile egg-shaped oval, originally built in 1950 and not for the speeds we reach there now. It's located in the Sandhills region of the Carolinas, and that sandy soil gets into the asphalt, grinds it up, and makes the track surface rough and bumpy. It takes full concentration to get around there alone, not to mention in a race with thirty-nine other cars.

I never felt any lack of confidence in my ability to get around that racetrack. I felt good. The last time I'd raced here, fifteen months earlier, we'd finished eighth.

What I was worried about were my eyes. As Greg Ives walked me through the plan—run a bunch of laps, come in for my tests with Dr. Petty, and head back out for more—and as Adam Jordan reached into the car and buckled up my window net, I was really conscious of my eyes. I tried to be mindful of my anxiety level and how that could affect my symptoms. But I was genuinely worried that when I got my car up to speed, and I was riding that high line up against the wall along the top of the 25-degree banking, with the G-forces kicking in and the car jostling around and me trying to stay focused on the path up ahead, that all of that would trip my head out again, wreck my gaze stabilization, and give me those bouncy eyes while I was blasting around the track.

That's how I steered through that first set of laps. I think I ran fifteen in all, and I ran the first few pretty tentatively. By lap 4, I could feel it coming back to me. It fit like an old shoe. I came back into the garage and Dr. Petty ran me through the same set of tests we'd done in Georgia four years earlier. The stick with the dot was moved into my face. My eyes stayed locked. I was given a straight line to walk. I walked that line like Johnny Cash. Dr. Petty shoved me in the shoulder to see if I'd stumble. I stood my ground.

Checked out, I went back out. This time, as soon as my four tires hit the blacktop, I could feel myself smiling inside my helmet. This familiar wave went over me that I hadn't felt in so long . . . I couldn't even remember the last time I'd felt like that. It was like, *Oh, yeah, there it is. Okay, Junior, let's go.*

I dropped the hammer.

I'd run 15 or 25 laps and come see Dr. Petty, he'd tell me I looked good, and I'd go back out again. Drive, test, repeat. I ran about 185 laps—250 miles—over the course of five hours, and if they had let me I would've stayed out there all day long. While I was on the track, Dr. Petty was calling Micky, Rick Hendrick, and NASCAR to let them know I was good to go. When I was in the garage waiting on the crew or Petty, I would grab my phone and text Amy about how well everything was going.

When we were done, Dr. Petty let us know that he and Micky were in agreement that I was cleared and that Rick and NASCAR had already been informed. We had a little celebration among me and the team. Man, it felt so great to be with those guys again. I had been with Hendrick Motorsports for nine years now, and some of these guys, like Adam and Travis Mack, had either been with me on this car for years or had worked alongside with other Hendrick teams or even for me at JR Motorsports. A lot of these guys had stuck by me during my long losing streaks, stood in Victory Lane with me after my biggest wins, and now, here they all were, on a cold day at Darlington, having waited out my recovery, working their butts off to have that racecar ready for my return.

We were also happy to be back together. It was a genuine moment and we recognized that, so we took a team picture and we made sure Bowman was in there with us. He'd driven in ten of the sixteen races I'd missed, and he was now a part of the team too. One day soon, it would be his team and this would be his car. When exactly that would happen was a decision for another day. But first I had a decision to make about 2017, and I wanted the team to make it with me.

I asked them to meet with me in the narrow hallway of the hauler, the team's transporter truck. That's how we do it when we hold team meetings during race weekends. I told the guys that I would be back in the car for the Daytona 500, now eighty-one days away. But before the Great American Race, we were supposed to run in the Daytona Clash. It's an all-star race and had been part of Daytona Speedweeks since 1979, when it was called the Busch Clash. Back then, the only guys who made that race were the guys who had won the number-one starting spot during qualifying at a race the previous year. I think it should still be that way and only that way. I reminded the team that Alex Bowman was the guy who'd won our only pole position in 2016, not me. I told them that if they wanted me to be behind the wheel for the Clash, I would do it. It was up to them. But my vote was to put Alex in the car. I also reminded them that we might be taking a risk having me out there because I wouldn't have had much time in the car at all before the Clash, and it might not be such a good idea to have me out there racing cold turkey in the draft at Daytona. What if I wrecked in a nothing exhibition race and it got my head cloudy again and I had to miss the biggest race in the stock car racing world? I promised them I'd be plenty ready for the 500 a week later, but the Clash might be too soon.

Every member of the crew took a turn sharing their thoughts on the matter. As they talked, I could tell they really liked Bowman. That made me feel good. In the end, they agreed to have him run the Clash and let me concentrate on the Daytona 500. I knew they would agree with me, and I'm glad they did. Alex deserved that.

The press release went out the next day, but I'm pretty sure the word was already out because my phone was blowing up with texts from people in the sport congratulating me. On Friday we had a conference call with the national media. A lot of the questions were about the Darlington test and how that process worked. But there were also questions about the plan past 2017. The reporters knew that I had one year remaining on my contract with Hendrick Motorsports and wanted to know what my plans might be. They also wanted to know where my head was. How was I going to feel when I got out there in the racecar in traffic at 200 mph with money and trophies on the line?

I gave them some really great answers to those questions. The truth was, I didn't really know.

I do know that winter produced some of the happiest days of my life. I was going back into the race shop on a regular basis for more simulator time with Greg. I was visiting with my teams and my sponsors and talking with them to reassure them that I was indeed okay. But deep down I knew that our little media Q&A after the Darlington test and my visits with my team and my sponsors, those were just dress rehearsals, a small taste of the questions I would have to answer when the season started.

On New Year's Eve at the Childress Vineyards in Lexington, North Carolina, I married Amy Reimann, and she became Amy Earnhardt. Finally. The ceremony was perfect. It looked like something you might see in the movies. It was so amazing to have all of our closest friends and family there that night, all in the same place. There were plenty of faces there who are plenty famous to NASCAR fans. There were also a lot of folks there that race fans wouldn't recognize, famous only to us.

After the ceremony, we danced and partied into the early morning. As midnight approached, everyone counted off the seconds that thankfully put 2016 into the rearview mirror forever. The new year was going to bring a new start and new season behind the wheel.

But I knew that 2017 was going to bring some big questions with it too.

CHAPTER 9

THE RETURN . . . AND THAT OTHER R-WORD

2017

As you know now, I had dealt with the occasional r-word thoughts a decade earlier, though those went away pretty quickly. In the middle of 2016 I'd had that testy conversation with Rick when our talk about a three-year contract extension turned into my tantrum. Prior to that I had kicked around all sorts of various exit scenarios, everything from signing that new deal with Rick through 2020 to talking with Jimmie Johnson about splitting a final year or two with me, giving us both a wind-it-down farewell plan.

I won't even try to recall the number of times I had conversations with Micky about retirement during my recovery. I would try to get him to tell me that I needed to stop, but he never did. Instead, he would say, "Do you still have the passion to race? Do you still want to be out there?" He was always aware of the pressure I felt, not wanting to let people down, and he would remind me that it was up to me and no one else. He'd say, "You have to do this because you want to do this. You can't go out there on the racetrack if you don't really want to be there, or you're worried about being there."

Of course, I wanted to be there. I just didn't know for how long. I had been so fully focused on getting well, coming back, and keeping my anxiety levels from getting in the way of those goals, I hadn't allowed myself to spend a lot of time thinking much further down the road than where I was right at that moment.

What I did know was that the condition of my brain was always going to be on my mind. Always. I was still reading everything I could find on concussions, especially how they affected former athletes over the long term. I would read news stories about people like BMX biker Dave Mirra committing suicide, or San Francisco 49er Chris Borland quitting football at the age of twenty-five because he was worried about long-term head injuries, or NFL-player-turned-convicted murderer Aaron Hernandez being diagnosed with CTE after his death. At the start of the 2016 NASCAR season, at the same time I was racing and keeping my secret notes, movie theaters were showing *Concussion* starring Will Smith, the story of Dr. Bennet Omalu and his discovery of CTE in Pittsburgh. Now, as we approached the start of the 2017 season, word got back to me that Omalu himself was saying that I shouldn't try to race again.

So I would read and see and hear all of this stuff. When my nonstop mind tried to process it all, I couldn't help but think, *Man, if I hit anything hard again, is this going to be me? One of these guys who acts normal one day and the next day he wakes up a different person, suddenly hurting other people or himself?*

When I would call Micky—and I still called him a lot—I would express these concerns. He told me that he understood why I would worry like I did, but he also assured me that even if I was in a crash that hurt me again, he had no doubts whatsoever that he could get me back to 100 percent. As much as I love and respect Micky, I've never been able to fully believe that. Not the physical part. I know he has the tools, science, and staff to make me better again if they had to do it. They've proven that twice already.

But when he said that to me, I didn't believe I could ever be back to 100 percent mentally. I'm not talking about brain damage. I'm talking about state of mind. There are scars there that I know will likely be with me forever.

As I'd expected, as Daytona approached I was asked a lot of questions about the two r-words, my return and my retirement. Every January we have NASCAR preseason media days in Charlotte and every February we have another media day at Daytona. In between, there are a ton of other obligations, from photo shoots with sponsors to sit-down on-camera interviews with the TV networks.

They all asked how I felt, if I was nervous about coming back, and if I was retiring sooner than later. Those questions only picked up steam after one of my longtime racing opponents, Carl Edwards, shocked the racing world and announced his retirement in early January. Carl is five years younger than me, and the previous season he'd won three races and was one of the four championship finalists. When asked why he was walking away in his prime, he mentioned me and my 2016 concussions. "I don't like how it feels to take the hits that we take, and I'm a sharp guy, and I want to be a sharp guy in thirty years. So those risks are something that I want to minimize . . . I think everyone in the sport paid attention to what happened with him."

"Him" is me.

I do want to clear up something about the weeks leading into the 2017 season. The NASCAR world is always full of rumors, and there were a lot of stories making the rounds that I had family and friends begging me not to get back into a racecar. That's not true. At all. I did have people tell me that if I chose not to come back, that was okay, and that they wouldn't talk me out of it if I did walk away. But no one ever said, "This is stupid, man. Don't do this." They all supported my decision, whichever way that went.

That includes Amy. She did several of those pre-Daytona media interviews with me, including a big one with my old teammate Jeff Gordon, who now works as a commentator for Fox Sports. She put on a brave face and explained to Jeff that no one in their right mind would ever come between a driver and his racecar. She meant it. She would never do that. The truth is, despite what some people might want to believe, without her and her hard work I would have never made it back behind the wheel.

But the other truth was that she was terrified. That's the word she uses now. That's the word she used when we asked her to describe her feelings headed into the 2017 season. I don't blame her one bit. Think about what I told you about where my head was, always wondering if I was one hit away from being hurt again, maybe even worse than before. Now think about how she felt. She still gets upset when she talks about it, even now, long after it happened. But you wouldn't expect that if you had seen her at Daytona that February. She was by my side, looking strong as a rock.

The most incredible lesson I have learned from Amy is what it feels like to be really, truly loved. More than that, what it feels like to be truly taken care of. What my mother did for me, while dealing with everything she had to deal with personally, that's true love. What my sister has done for me my whole life, that's true love too. To this day, Kelley has taken care of me like no other big sister has ever looked out for her little brother. But if you're fortunate enough to be married to the true love of your life like I am, then you know what I'm talking about when I'm describing what I have learned from Amy about love. If there's one positive that I can say came out of my awful 2016 experience, it's that it showed me Amy in a whole new light. We had already been together for years and had been engaged for a year before my big issues started. But if I hadn't had to endure my problems that year, I don't know if I would have ever fully appreciated how much she cares for me. My being out of the car forced us to do stuff together and have conversations that we probably wouldn't have had time for when I was all the time running around doing racing stuff. I knew, without a doubt, that if my rehabilitation hadn't worked and I had come away from it stumbling around and blurry-eyed for the rest of my life, she was going to stick with me, no matter what. That's true love.

When we got to Daytona International Speedway, Amy was right there by my side, just as she had been at every doctor's appointment and every doctor-prescribed workout in our garage gym. She was scared, but she was there.

Maybe I was a little scared too. But I was too excited to think about that.

Sunday, February 26, 2017
Daytona International Speedway

I started my eighteenth Daytona on the front row. We thought we were going to win the pole position in our first race back—could you imagine that?—but my teammate Chase Elliott snatched it away from us on the last lap of the day.

Race morning routines can be a huge pain, especially at the Daytona 500, by far NASCAR's biggest race. There is always a long list of appearances we have to make on behalf of our sponsors and, as you can imagine, more people than usual wanted a piece of me on this day because it was my first race back. For once, none of that bothered me very much. My time out of the car taught me to appreciate the little things about living the racing life, the kind of stuff that I'd just kind of tolerated and endured before. Even the things I enjoyed, like talking with the crew, I'd started taking for granted after a couple of decades of racing.

Standing on the starting grid at Daytona, I skipped right back into my prerace routine like I'd never left. Prerace shows are always awesome, with the fireworks, national anthem, and military fly-bys. At Daytona they take on a whole other level. I remember taking a moment to really pause and take it all in. I think I knew this might be my last one.

Just past the halfway point of the race, I was in the lead. The crowd was rocking. Everyone was in the middle of their pit stops, so the field was kind of jumbled up, and there was a wad of cars in front of me running through Turns 3 and 4. Kyle Busch's car let go when his right rear tire went flat, turning him sideways and collecting the two cars directly in front of me. I angled down the banking to try to avoid it, but the dang splitter started dragging the track, and I couldn't get turned fast enough. The nose of Kyle's car caught the right front corner of my Chevy. I hit him hard enough that my car hopped up on his right front tire, my nose got a couple of feet up into the air, smacked back down onto the asphalt and hung a right into the outside retaining wall. There it dot-dot-dotted a few times along the wall before I could gain control and steer it down pit road. We were done for the day, finishing thirty-seventh.

What received the most attention wasn't the wreck. It was what I did after the wreck. The race was red-flagged so that NASCAR and the safety crews could go out and properly clean up the mess from the six-car accident. When the red flag is displayed, everything is basically put on pause. The cars are parked, and the cars that need to be repaired can't be touched by the crews until the red flag is lifted. While I was sitting there waiting for the red flag to end, I ran a little impromptu eye test inside my racecar.

It's the same test I've already described to you a couple of times. I extend my arm out, point a finger into the air, focus on the tip of my finger, and then bring it slowly toward my face to see if my eyes remain locked on that point all the way up to my face.

People saw me doing that and they freaked out. It became a big deal. *"Aw man, Dale is still messed up, isn't he?!"* I regret not waiting to do it until I was out of the car and in the truck changing clothes or on the plane headed home, but keep in mind this was the first break in action after the first real racing I had done in more than seven months. It was eating me alive to know if I was okay. I felt fine. But I wanted to know for sure that I was. Being given a moment like this one, a chance to run a little test right there in the middle of the comeback race—at the time it felt like a gift.

By the way, my eyes worked great. That quick test only proved it. I had come back, run up front, wrecked, and walked away okay. That was as successful a day as one could possibly have while also finishing fourth from last.

But I ended up having to explain to everyone what I had done. My team, the media, my fans, everyone. We did our *Dale Jr.*

Download podcast the next day, and I explained it there just like I've explained it to you here. Also that I was mad at myself for drawing unnecessary attention to it.

That day I realized two things. First, as irritating as it might have been initially, the eye test reaction reminded me that I had an opportunity to use my experiences to educate people. Unless you've had a concussion and seen a specialist like Dr. Petty or Micky, how would you know what that eye test was or why I felt like I needed to do it? Now I had a chance to explain these things and maybe even convince someone who was suffering to go get some help. I'd known that before, but Daytona showed me the bigger reach I could have. You know, like writing a book about it!

Second, I think I knew then what I had always known, but Daytona made it official. I didn't have it in me to do what I needed to do to keep going over the long haul. I was thinking about my head. I was thinking about getting hurt. You can't race that way. You just can't. People have always said about racing, "Hey man, if you ever get scared, you gotta get out. If you're out there distracted, you gotta get out." I had both of those boxes checked. As February rolled into March and we posted a bunch of so-so finishes in races, I wasn't shaking those feelings and those distractions. I started worrying that I was wasting Greg's time and I was wasting the team's time. I didn't need to keep doing this.

I was really conscious of wearing my team out with all of it. Greg would call and say we had a chance to go tire test somewhere and I was like, nope, I'm not doing that. Forget that. That just felt like another great opportunity to hit the wall. A racecar driver, to do his job and to do right by the team, has to be fearless. That's where the speed is found and races are won. The great racing promoter Humpy Wheeler has always had a great line about my dad, that he "would drive his car where angels fear to tread and only the real racecar drivers can run." I'd never had a problem taking my car there. Now, maybe I wasn't so willing to hang out there all the time looking for that place.

Don't misunderstand me here. I wasn't just riding around the racetrack super slow and scared to death all the time. That racecar demands nothing less than full attention. It doesn't care if you have the flu or if your daddy died the weekend before. Big-ticket life events, stuff that happens to us all, they get lost inside that racecar. They have to. I ran 9,747 laps during the 2017 season, and during the vast majority of them I wasn't thinking about my head or how I felt or worrying about crashing. But when I woke up on the Sunday morning of a race, I was thinking about it, going through my wakeup checklist of, *Is this working right? Is that working right? Am I good to go today?* And if there was a crash on the track during a race, even if I wasn't in it, I was thinking about it.

In the grand scheme of things, that's not much. But it was too much. It certainly compromised the promise that I'd made to myself after I'd lifted my foot out of the gas at Talladega in 2014. Greg and those guys, they deserved someone in their racecar who didn't bring with them all those worries and concerns. They deserved someone who was worried about that racecar and nothing else. Someone like Alex Bowman.

We had just returned home from the fifth race of the season after having the kind of day that we had a lot of during 2017, finishing sixteenth at California Speedway after qualifying eighteenth and leading no laps.

I called Rick and told him that I wanted to meet with him, one-on-one with no one else in the room.

Wednesday, March 29, 2017
Hendrick Motorsports, Harrisburg, North Carolina

When we sat down in Rick's office, it was almost seven months after our talk in his motorcoach at Daytona. This time, there was no yelling or confusion. There were also no surprises. Rick says now that when I'd told him I wanted to get together, he instantly knew the reason that I wanted to talk. And he was right.

I told him that I was ready to retire from being a racecar driver.

We talked for an hour and a half. I cried a lot, and so did he. I told him that it was important to me that I honored the contract we had signed and finish out the season. He told me how much I had impressed him with my fight to come back and finish what we had started together a decade earlier. "I was so shocked he came back in 2017," Rick says now. "If it had been me, I don't think I could have done it. I know I couldn't have."

We did talk some business, about Rick's stake in JR Motorsports, the future of my team and Alex, and how we would go about handling the breaking of this news to our sponsors. But mostly we looked back over our time together. We talked about my dad. We talked about the decision I'd made in 2007 to leave Dale Earnhardt Inc. and join Hendrick Motorsports and how it had fulfilled the promise of our napkin "contract" when I was a kid. We talked about Ricky and how much we missed him. I thanked him for not giving up on me when I struggled so much during my first years with the team. To this day, deep down, I truly can't believe he did that. We remembered some of our greatest moments together, the ones we would have never had if he'd given up on me during those early years.

There were a lot of times during my recovery period when I

really struggled with those closest to me not being able to separate our personal and business relationships, being able to look me in the eye and share with me their genuine feelings about what I should or shouldn't do about my future. There were times when I struggled with that with Rick. And I know, being the incredible businessman that he is, Rick knew he could make a lot more money with me in the car for a few more years than he could make with me retired. But that day when he told me that the most important thing to him was that I be happy as a person, I knew that he meant it. As soon as he said that, I felt a whole new level of relief about my decision.

For a month, we kept that decision a secret. We decided on Tuesday, April 25, as the day I would announce my retirement, onstage at Hendrick Motorsports. We waited that far off because there was a lot to do to get that day together. In the meantime, I think there were only three people who knew at Hendrick Motorsports: Rick, team president (and Rick's son-in-law) Marshall Carlson, and Jesse Essex, who oversees the team's communications and media relations. At JRM it was Kelley, Mike Davis, and Tony Mayhoff, who oversees our marketing and partnerships. That was it. I had a list of people I wanted to reach out to personally and so did Rick, mostly family and friends. We moved very quietly. There aren't a lot of secrets in the NASCAR world, but somehow, this one never got out. It was so hush-hush that when Mike Davis and Jesse Essex had their first conversation to discuss the details of the announcement press conference, they spent the first few minutes just trying to figure out if the other one on the call actually knew what the announcement was going to be. Neither one wanted to be the guy who spilled the beans.

I have always had such a great appreciation for all of the people who work so hard just to take care of me and make sure I am where I'm supposed to be and do what I'm supposed to do when I get there. I've never been more appreciative of them than I was during this month. We all just went about our business at the track or at sponsor appearances and acted like everything was normal, even when it wasn't.

I don't remember being particularly stressed out during that month, but it is worth noting that the day before my retirement press conference was also the first day that I took down any iPhone notes in eight months.

Monday, April 24, 2017
Bristol Motor Speedway

The spring Bristol race was moved from Sunday to Monday because of weather. That compressed our schedule, but it also kept the media hounds off my case because they had to cover a race instead of wearing me out about the just-announced press conference. The weekend after my talk with Rick I had wrecked at Martinsville, but then bounced back to finish fifth at Texas Motor Speedway, my first top five of the season. Nearing the halfway point of the race we were running twentieth on a restart when my car just slid up the track and smacked the wall. We'd just had a pit stop and I noticed some smoke coming off the car. Turns out there was oil all over the place, including under my tires. With no grip, when I stood in the throttle to get going, it just took off and went wherever it wanted to go.

April 24 Bristol (Monday race): Slap wall when oil got on tires. Feel headaches right away. Headache stayed all night and was there when I woke at 4 am Tuesday. No balance or vision issues. Although my reading vision seems a couple more inches farther out than normal. Main feeling is just some headache/pressure in temples and head. No problem with environmental changes. No attitude issues or sadness.

I announce my retirement Tuesday so lots of emotions that are making any diagnosis difficult.

That afternoon after I had returned from Bristol, we were on the phone with our sponsors to give them an official heads-up on Tuesday's press conference. It was important to me that we talked to them and explained what was happening personally instead of just dropping a bomb on them Tuesday morning. Even if they had some idea of what was coming, I wanted them to hear it from me, even if it was what I was going to say to the world just a few hours later.

When I woke up for good that morning, I gave myself a personal eye exam, and that checked out. I closed my eyes and rotated my head to see if that would trigger any dizziness. All good. I did my walk-the-line "sobriety" foot test. That was okay too. Finally, I tested my balance in a dark room. That checked out too. I put on a suit and tie, and we headed out for Hendrick Motorsports, with Amy driving so I could go over the speech that Mike Davis and I had prepared.

Tuesday, April 25, 2017
Hendrick Motorsports

I met with my team that morning. They weren't surprised. Even if anyone on the crew hadn't known what I was about to announce in a few minutes over on the other side of the Hendrick Motorsports campus, they would have figured it out as soon as I walked in to address them in my suit and tie. I'm a T-shirt and ballcap guy. If I have on a suit and tie, then you know something is up.

I would love to tell you that I gave the team some awesome speech, like something out of a football or war movie. But I didn't. I just let them know that the rumors they had heard were true and that I was indeed about to go announce that I was retiring. I thanked them for their dedication to me and for their patience with me during my recovery. I told them that I felt fine, that nothing had happened that forced me to make a rash decision. They knew me well enough to know that already.

Then I promised the No. 88 team that they would be getting my 100 percent effort the remainder of the year and that, above all, we were going to have a good time. The part I had missed the most when I was out of the car in 2016 was them, and I wasn't going to waste a second of that between now and our final race in November.

I would also love to tell you that I was super nervous or super emotional before and during the retirement press conference itself. I wasn't. I was really proud of my opening remarks, the ones that Mike and I had worked on together. Maybe I was a little worried about getting emotional when I got to the sections on my family and Amy, but even if I was, it didn't happen. When we got to the Q&A part of the announcement, a couple of reporters did a little fishing for tears. They asked me if I had been emotional or sad, especially when I told my family members. But really, I hadn't. The only time I had cried was during that meeting with Rick, and that had been a month ago.

My overwhelming feeling that day? It was relief. Remember when I was keeping my head injury symptoms quiet for so long, but then felt so much better once I started sharing them with people, and Micky designed a plan? Having it out there and having a target to hit and to focus on—there was a huge sense of relief that came with that. I think this day was the same in a lot of ways. There would be no more speculation about when I was going to retire. It was out there, and we had a date on the calendar that I could circle and count down toward. My last Cup Series race would be at Homestead-Miami Speedway on November 19, 2017, and that was 208 days away.

My favorite part of that day, even more than the moment I walked off the stage, was when I walked outside the building where we'd held the press conference. Next door is the Hendrick Motorsports Museum, and every weekday it has a steady flow of NASCAR fans moving through, taking pictures of old racecars and trophies, several of them being mine. As the word had gotten out that morning about our announcement, a much larger group of fans had gathered around the museum than you'd ever see on a typical Tuesday morning. They were dressed head to toe in Dale Earnhardt Jr. gear, and they were waiting on me. I signed autographs and chatted with them. I took my time. I wanted to make sure I paused to enjoy this. One fan yelled to me, "Dale, buddy, let's make sure we enjoy this last ride together." I smiled and responded, "That's a deal, man." I was talking to him, everyone around him, and all of Junior Nation.

Wednesday, April 26th. No headache. No issues at all except feeling just slightly buzzed or hungover. Mentally slow. But otherwise zero issue. Later at work 10 am. Some headache when bending over. Wore prescription glasses till lunch and noticed some gaze stability issues while walking.

Sinus cold from Easter still there a bit. Went for a bike ride after lunch and felt a ton better during and especially after that.

There's something that had certainly changed about me after my 2016 ordeal. I was becoming a cyclist. As I've told you, working out has never been my thing. But after everything that I'd had to do during my rehab, I learned the importance of being in good shape. I'll always wonder if I might have recovered more quickly if I had taken better care of myself over the years. Well, I'm not running that risk again.

I had watched Jimmie Johnson haul his bike all over the place and had seen all of his social media posts about his rides, how he would jump on his bike during race weekend, sometimes between morning and afternoon practice sessions. I thought he was nuts. Now I wanted to try it. When I talked to him about it, he was very excited. He even gave me one of his bikes. I'm not talking about a Schwinn you would have bought at Toys "R" Us. This is Tour de France stuff, gear worth thousands of dollars. Jimmie just gave it to me, and then he started inviting me on his weekend rides, giving me pointers to get me started, and helping me with any rookie questions, no matter how stupid. I think that's all you need to know about the kind of man Jimmie Johnson is. He's got every excuse in the world to be a cocky jerk, but instead he's as generous a guy as you will ever meet. He wanted to help. He still does. I appreciate that so much.

Thursday, April 27th: Still some headache. Takes a while in the morning to clear my head before I can tell something is not quite 100%. Flew to Ohio for Nationwide with Rick. Felt ok by the time we got on the plane by 9:30. Still have some sinus trouble that may be causing the headaches on flight. Vision seems a little better today, smoother.

Friday, April 28th: Feel pretty good when woke up. Seemed all clear.

I would love to tell you that I have a huge pile of memories and great stories to tell you from the 2017 season, as spring turned to summer and then fall. But the reality is that the year really kind of flew by. Amy always says we had "senioritis," and that's the perfect description. Once the announcement was out there, it really took a load off my shoulders. Off the track, I was working with Rick and Kelley to make sure our sponsor relationships were going to have the best chance possible to continue even when I was no longer driving the No. 88 car. That's why you see that trip with Rick up to Nationwide headquarters in my notes. We also reached out to the racetracks remaining on the schedule and asked not to go too overboard with any farewell tour stuff, goofy gifts like rocking chairs and all of that. Instead, we encouraged them to find ways to support our charities through the Dale Jr. Foundation. Several of them were really creative and generous. That was very cool.

On the track, we had a couple of disappointing runs immediately following the press conference, but we rolled into June with a pair of top-eleven finishes at Charlotte and Dover. As summer started, it was becoming pretty obvious that we weren't going to be as competitive as we'd hoped. That wasn't just a No. 88 car thing; it extended throughout Hendrick Motorsports. Jimmie, the defending Cup Series champ, won at Dover, his third win over the season's first thirteen races. But he didn't win again all year. Kasey Kahne, in his final season at HMS, won the Brickyard 400 in August, but wound up with only six top-ten finishes and left the team at year's end. Chase Elliott was the most consistent of all of us, but he also went winless.

It was also becoming obvious that my anxiety over my condition was always going to hang over my head. Though it certainly never reached the level of 2014–16, there were moments along the way when my over-busy mind was working overtime.

June 7. Went to NBA Finals Game 3. All the noise and visual complexity ramped up my symptoms. Balance, and feeling awkward and disconnected. Dover race the weekend before was a very hard hit on my headrest and I felt like it shook my bell a little.

June 11. Mistakes on two shifts at Pocono. I have no idea why that's happening. It feels tied to my random feelings of dizzy/balance issues that happen sometimes. Turning around or any major motion of my head can upset my balance and understanding of level for a split second. This has been the case since I felt recovered.

June 25. Sonoma Raceway. Concerned all weekend about using curbs and how that's consistent with NFL linemen and constant pounding. Headaches Friday and Saturday. Saturday night there is nothing symptom wise going on. Just worry.

September 16. Chicagoland. Nasty bumps on this track. Immediately gives me headaches in the car during practice. Headaches last all day and during sleep at night. Practice 1 on Friday gave me nausea and disconnected foggy feeling after running a couple laps. It clears up after 20 mins. Even when ride quality in the car is improved, my vision never has recovered enough to handle the jostling of the car going over the surface of the track.

October 5. Charlotte. Practice crash. Right-sided the car exiting Turn 4. I notice my eyesight is affected. It's blurred and harder to read at a distance. Focus on objects takes an extra second. Busy environments are where visual issues are more apparent. My head had some aches. It's a low constant ache around eye sockets and temples. No balance issues. No issues in dark spaces. Not really foggy but do feel a little trapped, buzzed, annoyed, and disconnected. Felt slow and groggy this morning. Hoping to clear up as the day goes. Feel pretty clear by 1:15. Feel awesome Saturday evening.

Once you've experienced something like I did in 2016, even when you're feeling great, there are no more normal days. Normal, as in, you don't think about your body or your mind, and you just wake up, do your thing, and go to bed. Now, every little thing makes you pause and think, *Now, what the heck was that?*

I have always had a bad memory when it comes to short-term stuff, especially to-do stuff. If Amy needs me to run to the store to pick up a couple of things, if I don't write it down then I'm not going to remember it. That's probably normal, especially for a guy who leans on his phone as much as I do. But when you've suffered a head injury you're constantly questioning yourself. *Why can't I remember what Amy told me to pick up? Why can't I remember where I put my car keys?* Even if you know you couldn't remember that stuff anyway, you still end up wondering, *Dang, is this it? Is my mind about to go back downhill again?!*

Now, whenever I felt like that, I didn't keep it to myself. I would tell Amy. And I would call Micky and tell him. They would both talk me off the ledge, and I would be okay. Then, a couple of weeks later, we might go through the whole thing again. It's exhausting. But it isn't as exhausting as it was when I tried to keep it all secret.

You read all of that and you read those 2017 notes and you probably think, *Man, he must have been terrible on the racetrack.* But the second half of the season we actually improved quite a bit. I finished sixth at Sonoma and won the pole position at Daytona one week later, but that was really all there was to brag about during the summer. Once fall started is when we really picked it up. Starting October 1 at Dover, I finished twelfth or better in six of seven races. We scored half of our top-ten finishes for the season in October and November alone and won our second pole position of the year, in front of that Earnhardt-loving crowd at Talladega.

In the middle of all that, Amy and I announced to the world that we were expecting a baby girl. I'm telling you, it was a good fall.

All year long I think I'd kind of been counting down to the end, more or less wanting to get to the finish line and Homestead-Miami Speedway and call it a career. But that changed by the time we hit that stretch in October and November. All of a sudden, I realized that end was coming soon and I found myself panicking just a little bit, wanting to slow things down. It wasn't even about the races themselves—it was about enjoying the stuff around the races, like practice sessions and team debrief meetings, even sponsor meet-and-greets and going out to dinner in all of the host towns and cities.

My whole life I'd kind of taken those things for granted. A lot of the stuff that, honestly, I hated a lot of times. There was a time in my career—a lot of the time—that I would blow in right before practice started, run my laps, and then blow out of there to whatever the next thing was on the schedule. Now I caught myself hanging around maybe too much, showing up early and staying later, just trying to soak up every minute I could with my guys, knowing that my time was limited. Our cars were certainly better than they had been the first half of the season, but I think a big reason we had better results was also due to me and my new approach. There was an added intensity to every lap knowing that they were probably my last at every racetrack.

CHAPTER 10

SEND HER AROUND
ONE MORE TIME

Sunday, November 19, 2017
Homestead-Miami Speedway

I wanted everything during the season finale at Homestead to move in slow motion. Except, of course, my racecar. The week leading into my last race was a blur. We did a lot of media, but I was really conscious of trying not to take away much attention from the four guys who would be racing for the Cup Series championship, especially my bud Martin Truex Jr. I made no apologies about rooting for Martin. As I told you earlier, I'd played a big part in helping get him to the top level of NASCAR and I was very proud of that. I'm proud to say that I'd also had a hand in helping another one of the four finalists, Brad Keselowski, but Brad had already won a championship. If Martin could pull it off, it would be his first, and he'd been the best car all season long.

When I was asked to come up with a list of people who I wanted to fly in on race morning, I guess people expected me to give them a longer list, because everyone seemed a little shocked when I listed only six names. Yep, just six. On Sunday morning we flew in my mother, Brenda; her husband, Willie; my brother, Kerry, and his wife, Rene; and my bud Sonny Lunsford and his wife, my cousin Stacy. Sonny is my property manager. If you ever see anything cool that I'm driving or sitting on or partying in, Sonny probably built it.

During the race weekend I was asked why I was bringing in so few people, and I explained that they were my family, but I really have two families. They were my family from home. My other family was already at the racetrack. Kelley, L.W., and Mike Davis were already at the track, as were a ton of JR Motorsports employees. There were more than usual at this Homestead race because we had three cars in the final four competing for the Xfinity Series championship on Saturday. Pretty good, right? Among them was Elliott Sadler, one of my very best friends in racing. Amy, Rick—of course they were all already there too. You add all of them up with my No. 88 crew, and there's my family.

In fact, you can expand that out even further. Way further. After two decades of driving and two decades before that chasing my dad around racetracks, it's nearly impossible to find a race team anywhere in the NASCAR garage that doesn't have at least one or two guys working there who have worked with me or for me somewhere along the way. That weekend I tried to visit with every single one of them, even if it was just to give a handshake and a quick thank-you.

One of my favorite moments of the weekend came the Friday night before the race. Our sponsor, Axalta, had been very cool to let us run a red-and-black paint scheme that paid tribute to my very first full-time Cup Series ride in 2000. Meanwhile, Matt Kenseth was running his final race for Joe Gibbs Racing, and his sponsors let him run a black-and-gold paint job that looked like his car from his rookie year, also 2000. We came up together, battling for Busch Series titles back in the day and for Cup Series races and titles over the years. We've always had a bond, and while everyone was making a big deal out of my last Cup race, I didn't think they were making a big enough deal out of what, at the time, felt like it might be Matt's final race too.

We had arranged for a photo shoot with my car and everyone who had ever been with one of my teams, and we were going to shoot it that Friday night in the garage. I talked Matt into doing it too. So, there we were standing side by side, in front of our old-school racecars, while everyone who had worked on our teams lined up behind us.

At one point, when they were trying to get Matt's folks wrangled into position for their team photo, I slipped into the crowd of fans who had gathered around to watch. It was dark, and that made it easy to slide in there without being noticed, at least for a few minutes. I just stood there and smiled and took it all in. I'm a Matt Kenseth fan. Always will be.

On Sunday morning, race morning, I woke up a little bummed. I didn't expect that. I was so confident in my decision to be done at the end of 2017 that I guess I thought I would be like, *Well, this is it!* But instead, there was a part of me that was wishing we still had a couple of more races to go. That surprised me. I was worried that my team might not have felt included enough in all of the pomp and circumstance of the final ride stuff. And how much of that was there going to be? I was still really conscious of not stealing too much thunder from the guys who were there to win a championship.

The drivers' meeting later that morning was packed. I mean,

packed. A lot of racetracks will now have some kind of red carpet set up outside the tent or building where that meeting takes place and there will be fans lined up, but this morning there were hundreds out there, and it seemed like most of them were dressed in Earnhardt stuff. I worked the railing and tried to sign as many autographs as I could before I ducked into the meeting. By the time I got in there, there weren't many places to sit, so I ended up kind of in the back. That ended up being the perfect spot. I was recognized during the meeting and received a standing ovation, which meant an awful lot to me. Then, as the meeting wrapped up and everyone started to leave, where I'd ended up put me in the perfect position to stand by the door and shake hands with nearly all of the drivers, crew chiefs, team owners, and NASCAR staffers as they left to get ready for the race. That meant even more.

Immediately prior to every race are driver introductions. That's when the entire starting field is announced individually and you walk across a stage in front of the main grandstand, either to cheers or boos. My daddy used to hear a lot of both. I've always heard mostly cheers.

But I'm going to let you in on a little secret. I never could stand driver intros. It wasn't because I didn't appreciate the applause. I always loved that. Just, the whole process of standing around a half-hour before the race, then being up on what felt like a fashion runway waving when you just wanted to get to your racecar and get on with it—all of that used to drive me a little crazy.

For my last race, I positioned myself in this kind of hidden spot behind the wall near where everyone would go through a big doorway onto the stage as their name was called. I kept to myself and watched every driver walk by, just to take it all in, because I knew I was never going to do this again. And the whole time I was thinking, *Why in the world did I let this bother me so much before? This is awesome!*

There was always a long list of stuff I had to do as part of my job that I acted like was such a pain in the butt . . . why did I let myself think like that? I'll be honest, just like at your office or your church or wherever, there were certain guys that I was like, *Aw man, don't let this guy walk up and start making small talk with me.* Now I wanted everyone to interact with me.

My favorite moment was probably with Landon Cassill. He said he wanted to take a selfie, and that was cool with me. Part of my pre-race routine was to poke a little hole in my water bottle so that when we were standing around so long in the sun I could squeeze it and squirt a little cool water onto my hot, heavy firesuit and cool it down. I waited until just the right moment, and when Landon started to snap the pic I blasted him in the face with a shot of that water.

Those are the moments I knew I was going to miss.

We had qualified twenty-fourth, but that's not where they had us lined up on pit road before the race. They had my car parked at the rear of the field, all the way down in Turn 4. There were so many photographers down there that the racetrack set up some risers to keep them from having to push and shove to get their shots. I posed for some photos with Amy, my family, and the team. We all held it together just fine.

Then Rick and Linda Hendrick showed up. Once I saw him, I lost it. We all started crying. All of us. I joke with him now that I always have it under control until I talk to him. I don't know what it is about Rick that makes you cry. In this whole book I've told you about only three times that I cried, and Rick was there for two of them. He's this amazing human being, this shark of a businessman, and when you work for him you are part of this really huge machine.

But then, when you see him break down it breaks you down. You realize that you aren't just some piece of a machine. Those emotions are real. When a man cries, especially a man like Rick, it's hard not to cry with him.

He reminded me of our deal we'd made earlier in the week. If I brought my racecar home in one piece, then I got to keep the car as my souvenir, and he got to keep my helmet. That really was the goal that night. Nothing complicated or dramatic. Just finish the race running and in one piece.

Once everybody started crying, we kind of ran Rick out of there. As he slipped back under the rope to leave, he apologized. "I shouldn't have come down here. I spun out everyone's emotions."

Getting strapped into the car, however, wasn't that emotional. We kind of hustled through it because it was so dang hot. I wanted to get into the cockpit and get my cool suit hooked up and get my fans blowing. I also wanted my team in their thick firesuits and poor Amy, who was now almost halfway into her pregnancy, to get out of the blazing sun.

The one thing that I selfishly wanted to happen before the race was that I wanted all the guys on pit road, from every team, to shake my hand. When my father finally won the Daytona 500 in 1998 after twenty years of near-misses, everyone from every team ran out on pit road and lined up to shake his hand as he drove down pit road on his way to Victory Lane. That's one of the most iconic images in NASCAR history. I wanted to experience that for myself. Only, that day at Daytona they had all decided to do that for Dad. Today, I was deciding they would do it for me.

After "Drivers, start your engines" and the clearing out of all the non-crew members, I drove slowly down pit road as the teams were all getting their pit boxes ready for the race and stopped. I held my hand out the window and yelled to the first team, "Hey! Y'all are going to have to come out here and shake my hand!" At first, I think they were like, "Do what now?" but then they caught on and all the teams starting lining up. I saw so many faces of so many friends that I had made over the years. As my Chevy crawled along there, my whole NASCAR life was literally flashing before my eyes.

When all those teams shook my father's hand in 1998, that was them showing him their respect. Nearly two decades later, this was me showing them my respect.

I had fun in the race. We had the car running pretty well and spent most of the night running fourteenth, fifteenth, something like that. Coming down the checkered flag, I got into the fence a little, and it caused a tire to start going down. I hate that. It cost us about ten spots, and we finished twenty-fifth. But the goal of the night had been met. We'd finished the race running and in one piece. During the cool-down lap, I drove up ahead and found Martin Truex Jr., who had both won the race and the championship, and I put the nose of my car into the door of his. That was a love tap, a racer's way of saying congratulations, a high five with a racecar. Almost exactly one year earlier, he was running through my exercises with me at a hunting camp. Now we were celebrating the biggest night of his life and a milestone night in mine.

Now, normally if you've finished twenty-fifth after the race, you drive your car back into the garage and leave. But this was no normal twenty-fifth-place run. I drove into the middle of pit road and parked it right there. Amy, my mom, and Rick were waiting on me. I handed Rick my helmet and, yes, we were both crying again. I asked Amy what she was thinking when the race was over, and she said that she was sad for me because she knew I was done doing what I had always wanted to do, drive racecars, but she was also relieved because the final season had ended clean. I was okay. That's all she wanted, for me to be okay.

While we were talking and hugging, the strangest thing happened. A perimeter formed around us. I had expected—in fact, I was counting on—my whole crew to come out there and circle the car. What I hadn't seen coming was the crowd that formed around them. Race fans came pouring over the wall and onto pit road, and they surrounded the crew after the crew had surrounded me. At first it was just a few, then it turned into a few hundred. That made it difficult for one last member of the No. 88 team to implement a plan that he and I had come up with.

Andy "Squigz" Quillan was our team hauler driver, and I'd asked him to do me a favor. Back when I was first coming along in the Busch Series and later when I drove the Budweiser car, it was customary after a race win that they would give us a few cold ones to sip on while we celebrated the victory and packed up the truck to go home. I always loved that, just hanging with the guys after a race. I missed it. After we won the 2014 Daytona 500, kind of the capper for my comeback from the 2012 concussions, I surprised my team by having a stocked cooler delivered to Victory Lane.

Throughout the weeks leading up to the final Homestead race, I told the guys that we had to finish all the laps and be running at the checkered flag, because we had to have a beer together when it was over. It would be the perfect way to end our journey together. We put Quillan in charge of making that happen.

So, here was poor Squigz, trying to navigate this growing crowd with a hand truck carrying two giant coolers. Somehow, he made it right on time. Someone slung one of those coolers up onto the rear decklid of the car and distributed its contents to the team. Right there, live on NBC Sports, we toasted to the night and to my driving career. Squigz toasted with a Diet Mountain Dew. "Hey, I gotta drive the truck back to North Carolina tonight!"

It was kind of a surreal scene, really. Martin's championship celebration was happening just a few hundred yards away on a big stage, with fireworks and champagne and all of that. Meanwhile, there we were with the No. 88 car, sipping and laughing and taking our time. To be honest, even if we'd wanted to leave we couldn't have. The crowd of fans around us had grown to what had to be a thousand people, everybody holding up their phones and snapping pics. Every now and then one of us would hold up a can as a salute and the gathered crowd would cheer, but for the most part it was actually pretty quiet. We were just chilling out, me and my team, one last time.

Amy, Mike, and my inner circle of family and friends had stepped outside that circle, standing off to one side. Amy says that she was just watching and taking it all in. She hoped that I would take my time, as much time as I needed, and not hustle out of there too fast because I was worried about her or anyone else having to stand around waiting on me.

We were out there nearly an hour. I've heard retired athletes from other sports talk about life after baseball or football, and when they are asked what they miss the most they never talk about hitting home runs or scoring touchdowns. They talk about being with the guys. Not during a game but the other times, riding on the team bus or hanging out in the locker room. After being stuck on the sidelines for so long, and now with my guys and wishing this moment would never end, I understood what those other athletes were saying.

The fans were still there too. They didn't want it to end, either. But eventually someone braved the crowd and came in there and got me. There was a golf cart waiting to drive me back to the motorcoach lot, and Amy was already on it. I sat down next to her, fans reaching out to slap me on the shoulder and tell me goodbye. She took my hand and looked me in the eye.

"You okay?" she said.

"Yeah," I replied. "I'm great."

I was great. Even with all those people crowded around me and the lights and the attention, there had been no symptom triggers like there surely would have been just one year earlier. Even leaving my final Cup Series racecar behind me, I wasn't sad. I had paid tribute to my crew and my fans. Now I was with the woman who loved me, pregnant with our daughter, and we were on the way to see my family, who were waiting for me at the bus.

Man, I was better than great. I was happy. I had crossed the finish line. As that golf cart pulled away and down pit road, I was headed into my future.

DON'T BE A
HAMMERHEAD

The 2018 Daytona 500 was the first Great American Race without a Dale Earnhardt in the field since 1979, when my dad made his debut. It was also my first race back at the track as a retiree. So I was a little worried about how I might feel when I was hanging out without a car to drive. Then, the day before the race, I was moving through the garage and signing autographs when three men stopped me, a dad and his two sons from Maine. I was just going to sign their stuff and keep moving, but one of the boys spoke up. "Hey, man, you need to know something about my brother. You helped him."

Now they had my attention. They introduced themselves as the Rodrigue family from Maine. The brothers were Dylan and Cody. Cody explained to me that he'd suffered a concussion playing hockey that had gone undiagnosed. He had a miserable time, seeing half a dozen doctors, and none of them had helped him feel better. Then he read a story in *ESPN The Magazine* about my comeback that mentioned my visits with Dr. Micky Collins. The Rodrigue family contacted UPMC and scheduled an appointment. After several visits and treatments just like mine, Micky had cleared Cody just a few weeks before Daytona. He told me he had a new job as an HVAC tech and was about to go back to work. As Cody and Dylan talked, their dad, Steve, a big fan of my dad, listened with tears in his eyes.

"I just wanted to thank you, man," Cody said. "You saved me."

When we first started kicking around the idea of this book, people would ask stuff like, "Well, why do you want to write about this? Why do you want to share all the details of how bad you felt? Why do you want people to know you were out there racing a lot of times when maybe you shouldn't have been? Why do you want to try and explain what concussions are?"

The answer to all of those questions is the same. I want to help. I want to help people who find themselves in the condition that I was in and the fight that I am still in to this very day.

To be clear, I didn't save Cody. Micky did. Cody just needed someone to show him the road to a doctor where he could get help. I have sent a lot of people up that road to Pittsburgh. A lot of them are like Cody, who read my story or heard me mention Micky on TV or saw Micky and Dr. Petty during the press conferences when they sat onstage with me and answered questions. But a lot of them also called Micky directly because they would tell me their story and I would just hand over his number. Poor Micky, he had no idea when he gave me his phone number in 2012 how many people I was going to share it with. That includes several racecar drivers, but it's mostly been people like my new friend from Daytona—everyone from blue-collar workers injured on the job to youth soccer players to people who simply had a bad accident at home. That's who I'm trying to reach through this book.

Concussions make the news whenever they are attached to football players or racecar drivers. But of the twenty thousand patients that Micky and his staff see every year, pro athletes might make the headlines but they make up only a tiny percentage of the people who receive treatment. The Center for Disease Control estimates that more than five million Americans are living with some form of traumatic brain injury. Many have no idea. They suffer silently like I did, not understanding what's wrong and either too embarrassed to share their symptoms or too proud. They try to be brave and walk it off, to put a washcloth on it.

You think about how much differently we view injuries in the NASCAR garage now versus even just a few years ago. The way that doctors look at concussions, that's also changing all the time. Micky had said that the science is moving so fast that the techniques and ideas his office used for me in 2012 had evolved dramatically by the time I returned four years later. He says that if I had to come back for treatment now, the knowledge they'd be working with would be vastly improved again, even in that short span of time. And this is coming from one of the planet's leading specialists, a guy who is always on the front edge of brain science.

This applies to how concussions are handled at the racetrack too. It wasn't so long ago that NASCAR didn't really have any concussion protocol to speak of. Now, in no small part because of me, they do and it keeps improving too. In fact, just as we were writing this book, NASCAR and IndyCar both announced that they were adding new eye tests to post-crash driver checkups in the infield care center, aimed at making a better-informed first diagnosis. I was happy to see that they were being proactive, making a change to improve their processes instead of just reacting to something bad that happened. I think what their protocol is now won't even be recognizable in five or ten years from now, as we continue to learn and understand. I hope that the same is true for every auto racing series, especially at the lower levels, where the future stars of the sport are just getting started. They need to be educated on what they can do to better protect themselves, before and after head injuries.

If anyone at NASCAR ever wants my input or advice, I want them to know that they can call me anytime. That goes for the drivers too. When my old rival Kyle Busch was told of the new eye test he welcomed it and said, "A lot of times, NASCAR has to save us from ourselves." He's right. In the end, the real responsibility will always be on the individual to recognize that they are injured, to know that they need help. Even as the science changes, most concussions are self-diagnosed.

That's why, if you think you have suffered a head injury, if you read my descriptions of what I felt and thought, *Man, that's just like me*, but your doctor is telling you otherwise, go get a second opinion. If your doctor was right, then great. No harm done. But if they are wrong, then you are losing precious time that could have been used to treat what's really making you sick. And even if you had a doctor clear you, that doesn't mean you are totally in the clear.

In April 2018 I took a trip to Martinsville Speedway with my new NBC Sports coworkers, Rick Allen and my old buddy Steve Letarte, just to walk around the garage and catch up with everyone in the sport. During that visit I got a quick reminder that as good as I feel now, there is still work to do.

I hadn't been there just to watch the cars go around since I was a kid. As an adult I was always in one of those cars. So I walked down into one of the turns to watch those cars hammer by during practice. I followed them one after the other with my eyes. *Whomp. Whomp. Whomp.* Suddenly, my symptoms came raging back. I lost my balance and had to grab ahold of something to catch myself. Now my anxiety started ramping up. Could anyone see me? Was someone watching and thinking, *Dang, Junior still isn't right in the head*? I hid in between the tires that Goodyear stacks up for race weekends and totally freaked out. My mind was in overdrive. *I can't be relapsing, right? I'm married now! I have a daughter on the way! What if I can't be there for Amy and our baby because my brain had decided to quit?*

Eventually, I gathered myself up and climbed high atop the No. 88 hauler, hoping for some fresh air and a less intense atmosphere. I reached out to Micky. He, as always, talked me down. He told me that, while Martinsville was certainly not a new place to me, this was the first time I had been exposed to this specific environment since I was a kid. My brain needed to be reminded of what that environment felt like and how to process it, the noise and the imagery and the constant movement. It was just another exposure exercise. He said what I should have done was dig in and force my brain and eyes to focus up.

It was a reminder that, while I might be healed, I'm not entirely fixed. I don't know that I ever will be completely. That's why, sometimes, I still need help. And that's why, if you don't feel quite right, you need help too. After you get that help, learn from it. Do what the doctors tell you to do.

Several weeks later I was back at the racetrack, rehearsing with my NBC Sports crew during the 600-miler at Charlotte Motor Speedway. Our makeshift broadcast booth was in a suite high above the track, and we were standing, with no handrails. It set me off. I felt like if I stood, I would fall down through the glass. Then I remembered what Micky told me after Martinsville. I would take a break and sit down, then stand up and return again. I did that over and over, and each time my feelings lessened. By the halfway point of the race, they had disappeared again. Pretty tricky stuff, how the brain can adjust like that. I'd reminded it and retrained it, on the spot, just as Micky had challenged me to do.

On May 1, 2018, right in between my spells at Martinsville and Charlotte, Amy gave birth to our daughter, Isla Rose Earnhardt. I think about brain science, head injury treatment, and the way we react to the word *concussion*, how much all of that has changed during my lifetime and especially how much it has changed in the last few years. What will it be like when my daughter is my age? How much will it have evolved by then? It's good to know that there are some really smart people like my friends in Pittsburgh who are out there chasing the truth about what happens inside our heads.

So if you don't feel right, go see a doctor. See multiple doctors. Take an ImPACT test. Read whatever you can. Do something, anything, as long as you don't just sit there and suffer. You don't have to. Take it from me, because I tried that approach. I will always wish I had acted sooner. Who knows? If I had, I might still be driving racecars instead of talking about them.

Remember back at the start of this book, when I told you how I got my nickname, Hammerhead? It was for being stubborn. Don't be a Hammerhead. Instead, do this Hammerhead a favor and get help. Or if you think a loved one is suffering, then help them get help.

People like Micky and his staff, they are out there, eager to do for you what they did for me. To give you your life back.

ACKNOWLEDGMENTS

FROM DALE EARNHARDT JR.

There are many people to thank, both in helping me battle through the fog of concussion but also helping me tell about it. A good place to start is my family and friends. You don't go through the peaks and valleys of concussion—not to mention the process of deciding to change careers—without a deluge of support from those close to you. My wife, Amy; my sister, Kelley; my brother-in-law, L.W. Miller; and my brand director, Mike Davis, are just a few.

This book doesn't begin well without an incredible boss and race team. Not a day goes by where I don't feel immense gratitude for having Rick Hendrick in my life. And what a privilege it was to compete with Steve Letarte, Greg Ives, and everyone on the No. 88 Hendrick Motorsports team.

This book doesn't end well without Dr. Jerry Petty of Carolina NeuroSurgery & Spine and Dr. Micky Collins of University of Pittsburgh Medical Center Sports Medicine Concussion program. Those two men—and their remarkable staffs—were put on this earth to help people.

ACKNOWLEDGMENTS

This book isn't told well without Ryan McGee. He is a professional in every sense of the word and an extraordinary talent. To do this correctly required us to spend a lot of time together; not a second of it felt like work.

This book doesn't exist well with the fantastic W Publishing Group at HarperCollins Christian Publishing and also my literary agent, Mel Berger, at William Morris Endeavors. Thanks for taking a chance on me.

Finally, this book isn't important without people who have dealt (or are dealing) with concussions. Or setbacks. Or difficult decisions. Or heartache. Or conflictions. Life's hurdles come in a variety of forms, none of which are easy. You can prevail. Perhaps the words in these pages can help you. If so, it's why I wrote them.

FROM RYAN MCGEE

I would like to thank the staffs at JR Motorsports, Hendrick Motorsports, and UPMC for their willingness to answer countless questions at all times of day and night, specifically Mike Davis, Kelley Earnhardt Miller, Tony Mayhoff, Jesse Essex, and Dr. Micky Collins, who fielded the brunt of the requests.

Additional thanks to Steve Letarte, Brad Keselowski, Rick Hendrick, JR Rhodes, Doug Duchardt, Greg Ives, and the entire No. 88 crew for conversations that provided background, details, perspective, and insight along the way. Thank you to my longtime friends and colleagues in the NASCAR media center and TV compound, who did an amazing job documenting Dale's story as it happened.

Much appreciation to my wife, Erica; my daughter, Tara; and

my ESPN coworkers, all of whom showed great patience as I shoe-horned this project into my already busy life.

Also, thank you to Debbie Wickwire and her coworkers at W Publishing, Thomas Nelson, and HarperCollins for their guidance and, dare I say, friendship! And to Jane Dystel and her team at Dystel, Goderich & Bourret. I hope this is merely our first chapter.

But the greatest thanks are reserved for Dale and Amy Earnhardt, for entrusting me with helping them tell the story of the most frightening time of their lives . . . and for letting me see baby Isla in person before most of the world!

ABOUT THE AUTHORS

DALE EARNHARDT JR. is an American professional stock car racing driver, champion team owner, businessman, and television analyst for NBC Sports Group. He began his racing career at seventeen years of age with his dad, Dale Earnhardt Sr. He won consecutive NASCAR Busch Series Championships in 1998 and 1999 and the Daytona 500 in 2004 and 2014. Dale lives in Mooresville, North Carolina, with his wife, Amy, and their daughter, Isla Rose.

RYAN MCGEE, an ESPN senior writer, is a five-time National Motorsports Press Association Writer of the Year and four-time Sports Emmy winner. In 2007 he wrote the script for the documentary *Dale*, about Earnhardt's father, narrated by Paul Newman. He lives in Charlotte with his wife, Erica, and their daughter, Tara.